GARLIC THE mighty BULB

GARLIC THE mighty BULB

Cooking, growing and healing with garlic

Natasha Edwards

Photography by Peter Cassidy

FIREFLY BOOKS

A FIREFLY BOOK

Published by Firefly Books Ltd. 2012

First printing

Publisher Cataloging-in-Publication Data (U.S.)

Edwards, Natasha.
    Garlic : the mighty bulb / Natasha Edwards.
[160] p. : cm.
ISBN-13: 978-1-77085-101-6 (pbk.)
1. Cooking (Garlic). 2. Garlic — Health aspects. 3. Garlic. I. Title.
641.6526 dc23   TX819.G3E383 2012

Library and Archives Canada Cataloguing in Publication

Edwards, Natasha
    Garlic : the mighty bulb / Natasha Edwards
Includes index.
ISBN 978-1-77085-101-6
    1. Garlic. 2. Cooking (Garlic). I. Title.
TX819.G3E48 2012   641.6'526   C2012-900860-5

Published in the United States by
Firefly Books (U.S.) Inc.
P.O. Box 1338, Ellicott Station
Buffalo, New York 14205

Published in Canada by
Firefly Books Ltd.
66 Leek Crescent
Richmond Hill, Ontario L4B 1H1

Printed and bound in China by C&C Offset Printing Company Ltd

This book was developed by:
Kyle Books
23 Howland Street
London W1T 4AY
Editor: Vicki Murrell
Design: Louise Leffler
Photography: Peter Cassidy
Illustration: Rebecca Bradley
Recipe home economy and styling: Annie Rigg
Copy editor: Lisa Morris
Proofreader: Anne Newman
Production: Nic Jones, Gemma John and Lisa Pinnell

Disclaimer

The information and advice contained in this book are intended as
a general guide. Neither the author nor the publishers can be held
responsible for claims arising from the inappropriate use of any remedy
or exercise regime. Do not attempt self-diagnosis or self-treatment for
serious or long-term conditions before consulting a medical professional
or qualified practitioner. Do not begin any exercise program or undertake
any self-treatment while taking other prescribed drugs or receiving
therapy without first seeking professional guidance. Always seek medical
advice if any symptoms persist.

Contents

Foreword

Seldom in my experience has there been a better merging of author and subject. Natasha Edwards grew up on her parents' garlic farm on the Isle of Wight and has spent her entire life surrounded by the lore and uses of garlic (the mighty bulb). This delightfully presented book contains a fascinating store of facts, health remedies and delicious recipes. Garlic, as Natasha tells us, has been regarded as medically beneficial since the dawn of time, and I for one will certainly be drinking her garlic tea in the cold months ahead, along with her various other remedies. I am amazed to discover that there are 600 different types of alliums and a huge selection of different garlics, all with individual tastes and uses. The names are magic: hardnecks; softnecks; silverskins; purple stripes; elephant; ramsons; rocambole; bear garlic, to name but a few. As Natasha tells us, modern pharmaceuticals have diminished the reputation of garlic as medically effective. She doesn't add, but I will, that over-use of these drugs has reduced their efficacy and their repute. History has not disproved the use of garlic!

The main glory of this book, however, is, of course, the recipes harvested from all over the world and the far-flung places where garlic grows. Natasha's mother, Jenny, is a formidable cook and her daughter has clearly inherited this talent. The recipes are well and clearly written and, more importantly, they not only work but the end result is delicious. This book is an important addition to any cook book collection and an excellent tool for every avid cook. I recommend it to you.

Clarissa Dickson Wright 2011

Introduction –
garlic is great

How can something so healthy also taste so good? It's a shame we can't say this about all the delicious things in life but happily with garlic, we can as it has both – health benefits and flavor – in abundance. I grew up with garlic – on Mersley Farm, now popularly known as "the garlic farm" on the Isle of Wight – and so inevitably it has played a very big role in my life. And yet, incredibly, years and years of planting, harvesting, cleaning, braiding, cooking, tasting and talking about garlic have done nothing to dampen my enthusiasm for the affectionately named "stinking rose." I love garlic and all my family are what you might call devoted "alliophiles." The plant has a natural magnetism: it draws people in, amuses, excites and inspires and as you are reading this book, it's likely that garlic has already lured you in some way too. Perhaps you already add the odd clove to your cooking or maybe you are intrigued by stories of garlic's therapeutic properties. Whatever

your existing relationship with garlic, my mission is to encourage you to use more of it – for its wonderful flavor and its many health benefits too.

Medicinal marvel

Our ancestors intuited that garlic had enormous potential as a natural healer and these days scientific research is proving it all to be true. As well as vitamins and minerals, the cloves contain numerous health-giving sulfur compounds, of which allicin is the most potent. These are triggered into action when a garlic clove is chewed, crushed or cut, releasing its signature pungent aroma. They then set to work in harmony with the body to protect it against a variety of common ailments and more serious diseases. Millions of years of evolution have allowed the garlic bulb to perfect this self-protecting mechanism – all we have to do is consume it!

Garlic on the Isle of Wight

Garlic and the Isle of Wight are also two things that you would not necessarily pair together and so, like an odd-couple romance, I love the story of how they came to be a match made in heaven. My grandparents first moved to the Isle of Wight in the 1950s to take over the running of a mixed farm. My grandmother, Norah Boswell, was an avid gardener and also a great admirer of the inspirational food writer Elizabeth David who introduced post-war Britain to the rich world of Mediterranean food. Norah was inspired to conjure up the tastes of Italy and France in her own kitchen but soon realized that a zucchini, an eggplant and a garlic bulb were still considered alien specimens by shopkeepers in the local town. Ever resourceful, Norah cleared some room in her kitchen garden and began her search for good garlic planting stock. She soon realized that she did not have very far to go....

Garlic's association with the Isle of Wight had actually begun 30 years earlier when the island, due to its proximity to France, had been used as a base by the Free French Forces during the Second World War. Bill, a

farming neighbor of Norah's, had owned a pub in Cowes that was popular with the French fighters and, missing the tastes of home, they had asked if he might grow some garlic for them. Bill searched the island for planting stock but found none, and then he thought of a solution – friends of his in the RAF who at that time were flying Lysanders in and out of German-occupied Auvergne in Central France, delivering and collecting members of the Special Operations Executive (SOE). He persuaded a couple of them to slip a few bulbs into their packs and so the first garlic bulbs were brought back to take root in Isle of Wight soil and bring a Gallic *je ne sais quoi* to the streets of Cowes. Thirty years later my grandmother started her first trials with this very same stock – not enjoying much success at first, yet she persevered and soon had a flourishing garlic patch and an indispensable new ingredient that quickly became a staple in family meals.

A re-acquired taste

In the late '70s my parents Colin and Jenny joined the family business, which was still a mixed farm with livestock and corn. My father however, armed with a degree in Economics and a business background in marketing, foresaw the need to diversify into higher-margin crops and decided to turn his hand to growing and selling garlic to the British (no small ambition at the time!). The farm's first garlic crop was harvested in 1977 and, in spite of an inevitably bumpy start, held its course so that by the early '80s Dad's garlic growing was a fully fledged commercial operation. I was in my first years at school and most of my friends had never heard of, let alone tasted garlic. This was soon to change though as my older brother Ollie and I took great delight in leading our friends out to the fields and encouraging them to eat raw cloves from freshly harvested bulbs, giggling as the foreign flavor overwhelmed their

taste buds. I'm sure they weren't the only ones to think the Boswells were crazy, with their passion for this rather exotic foreign ingredient. It's been strange, and rather lovely to have witnessed how much times have changed since those days. Garlic's popularity has soared – way beyond my father's wildest imaginings – and we've taken it to our hearts. A kitchen with a bulb of garlic nestling somewhere in a pot or hanging in an elegant braid from the ceiling is as common these days as it was a rarity only 30 or so years ago. It's a staple ingredient, which we can prize for its flavor as well as its health-giving properties and I hope this book will provide you with many opportunities to use garlic and embrace its power.

Garlic farmer by Colin Boswell

It should be no surprise to me that my daughter, Natasha, having lived in a house in which garlic is a daily talking point, should have found it as compelling a subject to investigate as her father does, and now spreads the garlic word in this book, *Garlic: The Mighty Bulb*.

Garlic has an allure unlike any other vegetable or plant. I remember my first crop, grown from two sacks of virus-free bulbs from the Auvergne, which my wife and I had traveled to France to collect. We kept it, gently permeating the house, until planting time came in February. We planted an acre with it, on our knees, and followed its progress until that magical time which occurs in the late spring with the garlic of the Auvergne, around Midsummer's Day.

Nature throws a switch and the garlic bulbs, resembling spring onions, begin to expand. Given sufficient moisture they can double in size in less than a week. They continue to grow until, by mid-July, the effort of this growing spree makes them bend over and lie flat on the ground. The stem begins to wither as the moisture is withdrawn into the bulb and senescence, Nature's sleep, takes over.

The sheer pleasure in then lifting a fully formed garlic bulb is immense. The bulb has an unexpected weight to it. It hints at something powerful inside and, if left in the sun to dry, sheds its outer shell at a touch to reveal one of nature's jewels, a brilliant white sculptured bulb.

It seems so obvious to anyone who grows a good crop of garlic, that this is a force for good with powerful health-giving properties. It is no surprise that man, from the time he could communicate a positive or negative attribute of a bulb, scratched out from the earth, has invested this plant with a reputation that modern science (and my daughter) is now confirming. I was fortunate to have found early on in my life this plant whose study has been so rewarding and enriching in so many ways. Whether in an Alpine meadow in Kazakhstan or on a rocky escarpment in Eastern Turkey, the origins of the garlic plant we grow today have a long and strong connection to our own past.

The anecdotal life-enhancing knowledge that came from ten thousand generations' continuous close association with garlic, before our current experiment of perhaps ten generations, must mean that we continue to have so much to learn. This book will set you on that path. Savor the warmth of the mighty bulb.

Cooking and recipes

An essential ingredient

A beautiful package of healthy goodness and irresistible flavor, garlic is one of the world's most valued ingredients. In fact, it has become synonymous with so many cuisines that most kitchens would be bare without it. Its versatility and spectrum of flavors make it fun and dynamic to cook with and help inspire culinary creativity.

Over the years, our farmhouse kitchen has seen hosts of experiments with garlic – with varying degrees of success. My mother is an excellent cook and has always dished up wholesome home-cooked delights for her five children. Her food generally favors typical English farmhouse fare and, dare I say, were it not for her husband growing garlic for a living, it probably wouldn't have featured on the menu that often. However, with household finances in mind and fields of bulbs practically growing up to the kitchen door, garlic naturally found its place in our everyday meals and to me, food doesn't taste half as good without it.

For my mother, as for most of us, using garlic in food is primarily about flavor and rarely about health. Growing up, we experimented here and there with using garlic as a natural remedy, testing it on our cuts and scrapes or trying to fend off colds, but in truth we never really took garlic's role in our health very seriously. However, gradually we began to take note as scientists' investigations into garlic's reputation as natural healer continued to reveal just how beneficial eating lots of garlic can be. Consuming just one clove a day will not only top up your body's supplies of vital vitamins and minerals, but also provide it with unique sulfur compounds, which can go a long way in helping to maintain a healthy heart and help the body fight off infection.

"My final, considered judgement is that the hardy bulb (garlic) blesses and ennobles everything it touches."

Angelo Pellegrini, *The Unprejudiced Palate*, 1948

Buying the best

In order to enjoy the best flavor in your cooking, it's vital to use good-quality produce. It's great that garlic is so easy to come by these days and the local supermarket almost always has a good supply, though it's worth being aware that the kind of garlic on offer in supermarkets is generally not of the best quality – often grown from commercial cultivars that produce small bulbs with mediocre flavor. Once dried, commercial stock is almost always placed in a cold store at −3°C and drawn out for sale over a period of up to nine months. While in cold storage it keeps well, but once brought into ambient conditions, which mimic the arrival of spring, it will start to sprout within four weeks. Therefore, if you are looking for good-quality, long-lasting, flavorful garlic, it is best to look a little further afield. Growing your own garlic from sound stock is a very good way to ensure an ample supply of fresh bulbs (see Growing chapter, page 130) but farmers' markets, farm shops and online are also good sources, and often offer a wide range of varieties.

Top tips for buying good garlic:

*   Always buy the bulbs intact and without cloves missing. Once the bulb is broken up, its life is shortened.
*   Test the bulb for firmness – the firmer the cloves, the better. Any softness suggests the bulb is old and either won't last much longer or may already have started to go powdery on the inside.
*   Avoid any garlic with green shoots. If small green shoots have started to appear at the tip of the cloves, the garlic has already started to sprout. You can still use the garlic, but it won't last as long as a fresher bulb.

Green or "wet" garlic

Before garlic has fully matured, it can be harvested as green or "wet" garlic. At this stage, the papery dividers between the cloves have only just started to form, the bulb can be eaten whole, together with the stem. The flavors are milder than mature garlic and are really enhanced by roasting. Remove the very tops of the leaves as you would a leek, slice the bulb and stems in half, drizzle with olive oil, season well then roast for 30–40 minutes. Alternatively, green garlic can be used in a similar way as spring onions, chopped into salads, used in stir-fries or chopped and stirred through pasta dishes. Or you can try the green garlic pesto recipe on page 76. Green garlic used to be a farmers' market find but now you can find it in many supermarkets. Its season is from May to August.

Cooking elephant garlic

Elephant garlic is confusingly not really a garlic at all, but rather a member of the leek family. However, it does form a bulb that produces very large, garlic-like cloves, which are also edible. These cloves are mild in flavor and so elephant garlic lends itself well to being either roasted whole or treated more like a vegetable than a strong flavoring. If added too early on when cooking, the taste is easily overwhelmed, so it is best to add it at the last minute for a gentle garlicky note. Elephant garlic cloves can be sliced and added raw to salads or you can simply roast the entire bulb as you would normal garlic then squeeze out the flesh into a delicious paste.

Scapes

Hardneck varieties of garlic often produce scapes a few weeks before they are ready for harvest. The scape is the generic name for a flower stalk that emerges from the top of the plant, sometimes twisting and curling before growing straight up. These scapes should be removed before they start to curl in order to divert the plant's energy into increasing the size of the bulb. The harvested scapes should then find their way to the kitchen rather than the compost heap as they're edible and taste delicious.

Perhaps best described as garlic-flavored asparagus, scapes are great stir-fried, or sautéed in olive oil and then sprinkled with salt. They are abundant at the beginning of the garlic harvesting period and we usually serve them piled up on a platter as a sharing starter with aioli for dipping. They are also a wonderful crunchy addition to any stir-fry dish or as a topping for a risotto.

Storing

How you store garlic makes a big difference in maintaining its healing properties and flavor. The best place to keep it is somewhere dry, at room temperature and somewhere with good air circulation. Hung in your kitchen in a braid or grappe is the most convenient and attractive way to store garlic. See page 147 for instructions on how to make your own. Alternatively, store bulbs in a pot with ventilation holes. Avoid plastic to prevent mold. Only store green garlic in the fridge and do not freeze green or dry garlic as the texture will change. Properly stored garlic can last for months.

Preparing

The most exciting thing about garlic is how much its flavor varies according to the way it is prepared. Chopping or crushing a raw clove yields that distinctive pungent aroma and tastes strongest. This is because damaging the clove triggers a powerful chemical reaction that produces allicin, which is largely responsible for garlic's heat and strong smell. For this reason, garlic tastes milder and sweeter when cooked whole.

Peeling

Don't let the garlic under your fingernails hold back your garlic consumption! Peeling garlic can be fiddly if you're working with very small cloves, so the larger and drier the cloves, the easier the job becomes. If you intend to crush or bash the clove for cooking, the easiest way is to lay the blade of a large knife on top of the clove then press down on it with the heel of your hand to crush it slightly. This breaks the skin away from the flesh quite easily. Alternatively, you can buy a small rubber tube that peels the garlic cloves in seconds. Simply put the clove inside the tube and roll onto a work surface with the palm of your hand, applying pressure to release the skins.

Garlic fingers

When you're peeling, chopping and slicing cloves, garlic fingers become slightly unavoidable! However, there are a few antidotes you can try. Some people soak their hands in lemon juice or vinegar, and then wash with warm water and soap, or you can try rubbing your hands against stainless steel, which is often conveniently close at hand in a kitchen. Apparently the molecules from the steel and the garlic bond and remove the smell from your fingers. (This also works for onions.) When you're peeling garlic, you often find some sneaks under your fingernails so I'd definitely recommend a nailbrush.

Let it sit

In order to maximize garlic's health-promoting potential, leave it to sit for around 10 minutes after you have prepared it. This will allow time for allicin conversion while the enzyme is still active.

Crushing

Crushing garlic releases the maximum allicin and other sulfur-containing compounds from the clove, so it will result in the strongest flavors. There's a huge variety of garlic presses available and most will do an adequate job, but a better-quality garlic press will leave less waste and be easier to clean.

Crushing the garlic in a pestle and mortar will achieve a similar flavor but a slightly different consistency. If you cook crushed garlic, the flavor will become milder, so as the chemical reactions in the clove take up to a minute to occur, wait a minute or so before adding crushed garlic to the pan or a dressing to get the strongest flavor.

Slicing

Peeled garlic can be easily sliced with a sharp knife. But if you are preparing a large quantity you may want to use a garlic slicer, which is like a mini mandolin. Sliced garlic has a slightly milder flavor than crushed garlic. It's great in stir-fries and curries and can be lightly fried to create a sweeter, nutty flavor. Take care not to burn the garlic when you fry it though, as the flavor then becomes very bitter.

Green sprout

If your garlic is quite old and has already started to sprout, you may find a small green shoot on the inside of the clove when you cut it open. Although this is completely harmless and will not impair the flavor of the garlic, some people prefer to remove the shoot as it can be difficult to digest.

◆ Health burst

Allicin is the source of garlic's goodness and because it is partially destroyed by cooking, you'll get the greatest health boost if you use it raw or slightly cooked. Quite a few of the recipes that follow use garlic in this state and so preserve its optimum health-giving properties. I've identified these with a symbol (see above) so you can easily pick them out when some garlic aid is needed. However, don't be afraid that cooking garlic removes all the benefits as in fact it leads to other sulfur compounds being created which are also extremely beneficial to your health.

A shared taste

There is a global affinity for garlic, evidenced in nearly every cuisine around the world. A number of garlic dishes have become national and international favorites. Here are some of the most well known:

France

Aioli – originally a Provençal recipe, this garlic-flavored mayonnaise can be used as a dip or sandwich spread, or served as a sauce with grilled fish or meat.

Spain

Sopa de Ajo – a warming Castilian soup of garlic, leftover bread, stock, hot pimentón (Spanish smoked paprika) and a poached egg.

Italy

Bruschetta – toasted bread rubbed with raw garlic and drizzled with olive oil is the basis for this delicious Italian appetizer. Variations include toppings of tomato, beans, red peppers, cured meats or cheese.

Greece

Skordalia – used as a dip, sauce or spread, this is made by combining crushed garlic with a purée of potatoes, walnuts, almonds or stale bread that has been soaked, then mixing with olive oil to make a paste.

Romania

Mujdei – a white sauce with a very strong garlic flavor made by crushing garlic with salt and combining with sunflower oil.

Georgia

Khashi – a broth of beef entrails, lavishly seasoned with garlic, this nutritious dish is supposedly an excellent hangover cure.

Korea

Kimchi – there are many variations of this dish, which is essentially pickled vegetables seasoned with garlic, red pepper and ginger.

Thailand

Kratiem Dong – sour pickled garlic cloves served as a condiment.

Lebanon/Egypt

Baba Ganoush – roasted eggplant purée mixed with garlic, lemon juice, tahini and olive oil.

Middle East

Hummus – a mixture of cooked, mashed chickpeas blended with olive oil, tahini, lemon, salt and garlic, this dip is popular throughout the world.

Cooking methods

The recipes in this book use garlic in a variety of ways to create different consistencies and flavors. Garlic mellows with the cooking process, so adding garlic at the beginning makes for milder base flavors and, cooked slowly alongside meats, brings out wonderful base flavors. Raw garlic is more pungent than cooked. Crushed raw into a salad dressing will add a hot kick and adding it at the end of the cooking process results in strong, fresh overtones.

The conventional method of frying crushed garlic in oil forms a great base flavor for a large variety of dishes, including curries, soups and stews. When pan-frying vegetables, you may wish to slice the garlic to create a milder flavor and alternative texture.

To take the stinging heat away from garlic, blanch it by boiling in water or milk for a few minutes – or add whole cloves to stews or simmering liquids.

Roasted garlic, which has become popular in recent years, is quite different from raw or fried garlic. It tastes sweet and nutty, and squeezing the soft flesh from the skin is particularly satisfying. You can roast garlic in its skin, either as separated cloves or with the entire bulb intact. See the recipe on page 73 for the best roasting method

To really bring out the sweetness in garlic, try caramelizing the cloves. To do this, you will need to blanch the cloves a number of times before frying them in sugar or balsamic vinegar. See the tart recipe on page 26.

Keep it raw

A few ways to increase your raw garlic consumption and add a flavorful punch to your dishes:

- toss cooked vegetables in finely diced garlic and butter or olive oil
- add crushed garlic to salad dressings and cold sauces
- for a quick garlic mayonnaise, simply crush garlic into your normal mayonnaise
- sprinkle finely diced garlic over sliced tomatoes
- add chopped garlic to tomato or fruity salsas to accompany cold meats or cheeses
- for cheese on toast with a kick, place finely sliced garlic under the cheese

Recipes

Starters and Soups

Caramelized Garlic and Tomato Tarte Tatin
Ceviche ♠
Patatas Bravas
Garlic, Onion and Thyme Frittata
Sautéed Asparagus
Vietnamese Chicken Broth with Noodles
Garlic Bloody Mary ♠
Gazpacho ♠
Chowder
Bruschetta ♠
Avocado Garlic Prawns
Scallops with Lemon, Garlic and Spring Onions
Zucchini Fritters
Garlic, Cumin and Beetroot Fritters

Sides and Salads

Braised Red Cabbage with Garlic
Marinated Minty Garlic Carrots
Roasted Garlic Potatoes
Garlic Mashed Potato
Oak-smoked Garlic Dauphinoise
Spicy Purple Sprouting Broccoli
Salt and Pepper Squid with Aioli
Warm Lentil and Halloumi Salad ♠
Som Tam ♠

Mains

Chicken with 40 Garlic Cloves
Spaghetti Carbonara
Garlic Mushroom Pizza

Roasted Butternut Squash and Garlic Risotto
Asian Fish Parcel
Spicy Beef, Garlic and Scapes Stir-Fry
Barbecued Garlic and Lime Snapper
Brazilian Fish Stew – "Moqueca"
Slow Lamb with Mint Yogurt Sauce
Roast Garlic Chicken
Spicy Chickpea Curry
Tandoori Chicken

Dips, Sauces and Dressings

Aïoli ♠
The Garlic Farm Classic Hummus ♠
The Best Whole Roasted Garlic
Cucumber Kimchi ♠
Pickled Garlic with Lemon and Limes
Classic Pesto ♠
Green Garlic Pesto ♠
Classic Vinaigrette ♠
Garlic and Coriander Yogurt Dressing ♠
Moroccan Dressing
Salsa Verde ♠
Garlic Spread ♠
Hot Tomato Salsa ♠
Tzatziki ♠

Breads

Garlic and Rosemary Focaccia
The Very Best Cheesy Garlic Bread
The Garlic Farm Toasted Ciabatta

♠   Recipes with this symbol contain raw garlic

Caramelized garlic and tomato tarte tatin

This variation on the traditional tarte tatin melts in the mouth and makes an impressive dinner-party starter or summer lunch dish.

For the caramelized garlic:
3–4 garlic bulbs, cloves peeled but left whole
olive oil
200 ml (1 cup) water
15 ml (1 tablespoon) balsamic vinegar
10 ml (2 teaspoons) light brown sugar
sprig of rosemary, finely chopped
sprig of thyme, finely chopped (plus sprig to garnish)
5 ml (1 teaspoon) salt

For the tomatoes:
olive oil
4 ripe plum tomatoes, cut lengthways
  (or a basket of ripe cherry tomatoes, halved)
15 ml (1 tablespoon) light brown sugar
salt
freshly ground black pepper

For the pastry:
Ready-rolled puff pastry sheet, cut to fit over
  a 20 cm (8 in) ovenproof frying pan (make an outline with
  the pan, then remove and cut slightly inside the outline)
1 egg, beaten

To garnish:
250 g (½ lb) feta cheese, crumbled
sprigs of thyme

Serves 6

1. Preheat the oven to 375°F.
2. Put the garlic cloves in a small pan with water to cover and bring to a boil. Boil for 3 minutes then drain and dry the cloves and the pan.
3. Return the garlic to the pan along with approximately 30–45 ml (2–3 tablespoons) of olive oil and fry for a further 3 minutes. Add the water and balsamic vinegar and boil for 10 minutes, or until most of the liquid has evaporated.
4. In the meantime, prepare the tomatoes. Pour a glug of olive oil onto a large plate and mix in the brown sugar and plenty of salt and pepper. Place the tomatoes, cut side down, into the oil mixture and make sure each face is well covered.
5. Heat approximately 30–45 ml (2–3 tablespoons) of olive oil in the ovenproof frying pan and transfer the tomatoes, cut side down, into the pan. Fry for about 5 minutes, or until they start to go sticky, then remove from the heat.
6. By now most of the liquid should have evaporated from the garlic cloves. Add the sugar, herbs and salt, and continue to fry until the cloves begin to turn light brown. Remove from the heat then transfer the cloves to the frying pan and arrange around the tomatoes.
7. Place the ready-rolled puff pastry sheet over the tomatoes and garlic, tucking the edges of the pastry neatly into the pan. Brush with the beaten egg then place in the oven for about 25 minutes, or until golden brown. Remove from the oven and cool slightly.
8. Take a large heatproof serving plate and place over the pan. Protecting your hands with oven mitts and holding the plate and pan firmly together, carefully flip the pan and the plate, then lift off the pan.
9. Sprinkle with the feta cheese and garnish with a thyme sprig or two. Serve with arugula or watercress.

Ceviche 🧄

A Latin American classic, ceviche is traditionally made with raw fish marinated in citrus juices and other flavorings, which depend on the regional variation. The acidity of the juice changes the chemical structure of the fish in a similar way to cooking, but leaves it with a wonderfully fresh texture and taste. For me, this dish is all about the incredible "zing" on the palate and so I like to add plenty of chili, garlic and cayenne.

400 g (1lb) Sea bass, sole fillets or other very fresh white fish, skinned and deboned
1 small red onion, very finely sliced
1 celery stick, very finely sliced
1–2 red chilies, deseeded and finely sliced
5 ml (1 teaspoon) cayenne pepper
2 garlic cloves
juice of 3 limes
juice of 1 lemon
a handful of coriander, roughly chopped
a handful of mint, roughly chopped
sea salt

Serves 4 as an appetizer

1. Make sure the fish fillets are completely bone- and skin-free, then slice them across the grain into 1 cm (½ in-) thick pieces

2. Place the fish in a large bowl and add the onion, celery, chilies and cayenne. Crush in the garlic and pour over the citrus juices, carefully turning the ingredients with a wooden spoon to mix them thoroughly. Make sure the fish is completely covered in citrus juice.

3. Place the bowl in the fridge for at least 2 hours to allow the fish to "cook" in the marinade. You will be able to tell when it's ready as the fish flesh will have become opaque.

4. Stir in the coriander and mint, sprinkle with salt and serve immediately on one large sharing plate or in small dishes with the juices from the bottom of the bowl poured over.

COOK'S TIP

You can use pretty much any firm, muscly fish. Sea bass, sole and pollack all work well. Crucially, the fish must be very fresh and from a sustainable source.

Patatas bravas

The Spanish are great garlic lovers and much of their food takes full advantage of garlic flavors. There are many variations of this classic potato and tomato dish, but the flavors in this version will take you straight to Barcelona. It's a great accompaniment to other tapas or it can be served as an appetiser washed down with a well-chilled cerveza. This dish also works well topped with a dollop of aïoli (see page 71).

450 g (1 lb) potatoes
45 ml (3 tablespoons) olive oil

For the tomato sauce:
olive oil
2 small onions, finely chopped
1 fresh chili, finely chopped
3 garlic cloves, finely chopped
15 ml (1 tablespoon) tomato purée
400 g (1 lb) can chopped tomatoes
10 ml (2 teaspoons) sweet smoked paprika
  (or sweet paprika)
5 ml (1 teaspoon) salt
5 ml (1 teaspoon) sugar
chopped chives or aioli (page 71), to serve

Makes 4–6 small servings

1. Preheat the oven to 375°F.
2. Peel the potatoes and dice them into 2 cm (1 in) thick.
3. Heat 30–45 ml (2–3 tablespoons) of olive oil in a roasting pan until hot. Carefully place the potatoes in the pan, turning them in the oil until coated. Place in the oven and roast for 45 minutes.
4. In the meantime, make the tomato sauce. Heat the olive oil in a heavy-based pan and gently fry the onions for about 5 minutes, until translucent. Add the chili and fry for a further 2 minutes before adding the garlic, tomato purée, chopped tomatoes, sweet smoked paprika, salt and sugar. Stir well then simmer for 20 minutes until the sauce thickens.
5. When the potatoes are crisp and golden, remove from the oven, place in a large serving dish, pour on the tomato sauce and serve immediately with a sprinkling of chopped chives or a spoonful of aïoli for an extra garlic punch.

Garlic, onion and thyme frittata

This flavorful Italian omelet borrows potatoes from the Spanish tortilla, and is delicious as an antipasto or a simple Sunday-night dinner. Serve with a fresh, crunchy salad, drizzled with classic vinaigrette (see page 79).

2 large potatoes, peeled and sliced
about a ½ inch thick
30 ml (2 tablespoons) olive oil
30 ml (2 tablespoons) butter
4 small onions, or 2 large, thinly sliced
a large handful of fresh thyme sprigs, leaves only,
plus extra sprigs to garnish
3 garlic cloves
6 eggs
salt
freshly ground black pepper

Serves 4 as a main or 6 as an antipasto

1. Bring a pan of salted water to a boil and blanch the sliced potatoes for 3 minutes. Take care not to overcook them or they will fall apart in the frying pan. Drain in a colander to allow the steam to escape and set aside.

2. Heat the oil and butter in a non-stick frying pan then add the onions and fry over low heat for 5 minutes, stirring occasionally. Add the thyme leaves, crush in the garlic with a pinch of salt and cook for a further 2 minutes.

3. Add the potatoes to the pan, carefully turning them to coat in the oil and butter. Add more oil if necessary. Cook for a further 5 minutes on medium heat.

4. Meanwhile, beat the eggs with a pinch of salt and some freshly ground black pepper then pour the egg mixture into the pan.

5. Cook on low heat until the frittata starts to come away from the sides of the pan, then place the pan under the grill until the top of the frittata has browned slightly. The perfect frittata should be golden brown on the outside and slightly soft inside.

6. Serve the frittata directly from the pan or, if you're feeling confident, slide it out of the pan onto a plate and garnish with a couple of thyme sprigs.

Sautéed asparagus

At The Garlic Farm we are proud to often be the first in the country to harvest our own asparagus, usually around mid-April. Cook it with garlic and you've got yourself a plate full of healing food. And did I mention how delicious this dish tastes? By pan-frying, the flavors of the asparagus are enhanced and the garlic brings an extra edge. Serve with aioli (page 71) for dipping.

a large bunch of asparagus
olive oil
2–3 garlic cloves, crushed
sea salt
freshly ground black pepper
aioli (page 71), to serve

1. Trim the asparagus by removing the woody parts of the stems.
2. Heat 15 ml (1 tablespoon) of olive oil in a frying pan then add enough asparagus spears to cover the bottom of the pan. Sauté on medium heat for about 5 minutes before adding the garlic and seasoning.
3. Continue to sauté until the spears have turned bright green and have started to bend at the tips. Remove and repeat the process with the remainder of the asparagus.
4. Serve on a large sharing plate with a bowl of aioli for dipping.

ASPARAGUS FOR ARTHRITIS

My grandmother comes into the farm shop every morning during the asparagus season to collect her daily dose of fresh spears, which she has always claimed relieve her joint pain. I was somewhat skeptical until I read that, as well as being an excellent source of vitamin K and folate (a B-complex vitamin), asparagus contains high levels of anti-inflammatory nutrients and antioxidants.

Vietnamese chicken broth with noodles

Warming, invigorating, low-fat and incredibly tasty, I love to eat this soup any day; although it's particularly good for anyone with a cold. You can adjust the chili to taste.

750 ml (3 cups) chicken stock

1 packet instant miso soup

4 garlic cloves

a thumb-sized piece of ginger, cut into matchsticks

1–2 red chilies, deseeded and finely sliced

2 skinless chicken breasts

7.5 ml (½ tablespoon) sunflower oil

sea salt

freshly ground black pepper

100 g (¼ lb) egg noodles

2 bok choy, chopped

15 ml (1 tablespoon) soy sauce

juice of ½ lime

2 spring onions, sliced

a large handful of coriander

Serves 4

1. In a saucepan, heat the stock until simmering then remove from the heat and add the miso, stirring until dissolved. While the stock is still hot, finely chop 2 garlic cloves and add to the stock with all the ginger and chilies. Cover with a lid and leave to infuse.

2. Using a sharp knife, score the chicken breasts deeply 3–4 times across the top, then brush with sunflower oil and crush a garlic clove over each one, rubbing it into the meat. Fry for a few minutes on each side until browned but not completely cooked through.

3. Place the chicken on a chopping board and slice into strips. Add the chicken, noodles and chopped bok choy to the infused stock, return to the heat and simmer for a few minutes, until the noodles and chicken are cooked.

4. Add the soy sauce and lime juice and serve immediately in large bowls with a spring onion and coriander sprinkled on top. Eat with chopsticks for the noodles and a spoon to scoop up the broth.

Garlic bloody Mary

The wicked combination of garlic, tomatoes and vodka makes for a punchy cocktail or "hair-of-the-dog" concoction. Perhaps not the healthiest way to consume your daily dose of garlic, but definitely a fun means of testing the wonder herb's reputation as a hangover cure. Alternatively, omit the vodka and drink your Garlic Virgin Mary guilt-free. Without vodka it's still a great way to increase your raw garlic intake. Prepare ahead and refrigerate overnight to get the best flavors.

750 ml (3 cups) tomato juice
juice of 1 lemon
juice of 1 lime
15 ml (1 tablespoon) freshly grated horseradish
15 ml (1 tablespoon) Worcestershire sauce
2 garlic cloves, crushed
5 ml (1 teaspoon) Tabasco
salt
freshly ground black pepper to taste
premium vodka
4 celery sticks

Makes 4 tall glasses

1. Place all the ingredients, apart from the seasoning and vodka, in a blender and combine well. Season to taste then refrigerate until thoroughly chilled. The flavor improves the longer you leave it, so try to leave for at least 1 hour or overnight, if possible. This virgin mixture will keep in the fridge for a week so.

2. Put a few ice cubes in each glass, pour in an ounce (or two) of vodka, then top with the Garlic Bloody Mary mixture. Alternatively, pour the virgin mixture without the alcohol, either straight or on the rocks. Serve with a stick of celery in each glass.

Garlic & shots

If there is a darker, earthier side to garlic, then Garlic & Shots, the bar/restaurant run by the Swedish Olsson brothers in London's Soho, certainly captures it well. They combine wonderfully garlicky dishes with a choice of 101 flavored shots, served by waiters with a definite rock-and-roll attitude. It always makes me feel as though I should be wearing all black, heavy boots and more eyeliner. Designed for the garlic freak rather than the health freak, it certainly delivers on the promise of leaving its diners feeling as if they have been "marinated in garlic." The recipe for their signature "Bloodshot" is a closely guarded secret, apparently buried so deep behind one of the decorative coffins in the dark basement bar, it would take a very brave soul to find it.

Gazpacho ♠

Hot summer lunches are an ideal time to serve this very flavorful and refreshing, cold soup. It can be difficult to get raw garlic into your diet and this is an excellent option. If the weather is very hot, or if you haven't had time to chill the soup well, you can just add a few ice cubes before serving, as the Spaniards do.

1 kg (2 lbs) very ripe, good-quality tomatoes, roughly chopped
2 green onions, chopped
3 garlic cloves
1 large cucumber, chopped
75 ml (3 tablespoons) olive oil
juice of 1 lemon
30 ml (2 tablespoons) sherry vinegar
a handful of fresh basil leaves, finely chopped
a few stems of fresh flat-leaf parsley, finely chopped

For the garnish:
2 slices of white bread, cubed
olive oil, for frying
½ red pepper, finely diced
cucumber, finely diced
salt
pepper

Serves 6

1. Put the tomatoes, green onions, garlic and most of the cucumber (retain a small amount for the garnish) into a blender and blend until smooth. Pass through a fine sieve to remove most of the pulp.
2. Put the mixture back in the blender and slowly add the olive oil, lemon juice and sherry vinegar until combined before adding the basil and parsley. Be careful not to blend the herbs for too long as you want them to remain finely chopped, not puréed. Chill in the fridge.
3. To make the garnish, gently fry the bread in a little olive oil to make croûtons. To serve, season the gazpacho well before transferring it to bowls and topping with the chopped vegetables and croûtons.

COOK'S TIP

For those wishing to reduce their salt intake, garlic makes a great alternative. It adds substantial flavor to your cooking and means you'll need to use far less salt.

The secret to a great gazpacho is to use really ripe, premium tomatoes. Big, plump, fleshy ones are the best as they have fewer seeds, but anything sweet and delicious will help to produce a tasty soup.

Chowder

Garlic often complements culinary traditions in a way we wouldn't always imagine possible. This seaside treat is enhanced by the addition of crushed garlic.

30 ml (2 tablespoons) butter

200 g (½ lb) smoked bacon

1 onion, finely chopped

1 leek, sliced

4 garlic cloves

2 large potatoes, diced small

500 ml (2 cups) milk

1 bay leaf

10 ml (2 teaspoons) vegetable bouillon powder

200 g (½ lb) coley or pollack fillet or other white fish, skin removed, roughly chopped

2 fresh corn cobs, kernels sliced off

juice of 1 lemon

salt

freshly ground black pepper

a handful of fresh parsley, chopped

Serves 4–6

1. In a large saucepan, melt the butter over medium heat then add the bacon and sauté for a few minutes to release the fat.
2. Add the onion, leek and crush in the garlic then fry gently for 5 minutes, or until the onion and leek have softened. Add the potatoes and sauté for a further 5 minutes.
3. Add the milk, bay leaf and stock to the pan and cook for about 10 minutes, or until the potatoes have softened. Add the fish and corn and simmer for 2–3 minutes until the fish is cooked through.
4. Squeeze in the lemon juice and season to taste, bearing in mind you will need very little salt as the bacon and lemon add plenty of flavor.
5. Ladle the soup into warmed deep bowls, garnish with chopped parsley and serve with large chunks of crusty bread on the side.

Bruschetta 🧄

This classic Italian antipasto is a delicious and simple way to include raw garlic in your diet. Any good-quality, fresh bread can be used, though I prefer ciabatta, and you can try adding different toppings, such as pesto, cheese, anchovies, cured meats or grilled vegetables.

1 small ciabatta loaf, cut diagonally into 2 cm (1 in) slices
extra virgin olive oil
4 garlic cloves, peeled
6 very ripe vine tomatoes, diced
a small handful of fresh basil leaves, torn
sea salt
freshly ground black pepper

Serves 4

1. Brush each side of the ciabatta slices with olive oil then toast under the grill on both sides.
2. While the bread is still hot, rub with the raw garlic cloves, top with the chopped tomatoes and basil leaves then drizzle with olive oil and season well.

Avocado garlic prawns

This combination is packed full of goodness and makes a very easy starter or lunch dish.

30 ml (2 tablespoons) butter
500 g (1 lb) raw fresh prawns, peeled, deveined
3 garlic cloves
5 ml (1 tablespoon) sweet chili sauce
2 ripe avocados, peeled, halved, stones removed
juice of 1 lemon
salt
freshly ground black pepper
a bunch of fresh chives, finely chopped, to garnish

Serves 4

1. Heat the butter in a heavy-based frying pan or wok on high heat. Throw in the prawns, quickly crush in the garlic, then stir until the prawns are cooked through. Once cooked, stir through the sweet chili sauce.
2. Place half an avocado on each plate and top with the cooked prawns. Squeeze plenty of lemon juice over the prawns, season with salt and freshly ground pepper, then sprinkle with chopped chives.

Scallops with lemon, garlic and green onions

By marinating the scallops before cooking, the garlic permeates the fish rather than being lost during the cooking process. These little flavor bursts can be served alone as a starter or, if you increase the quantities and serve with wild rice, enjoyed as a main course.

2 lemons, squeezed and rinds (keep the juice)

50 ml (3 tablespoons) extra virgin olive oil

4 large garlic cloves

12 fresh scallops, roes removed

30 ml (2 tablespoons) sunflower oil, for frying

sea salt and freshly ground black pepper

2 green onions, finely sliced

Serves 4 as a starter

1. In a bowl, mix the lemon juice and rind (reserving a few strips of rind for the garnish), whisk in the olive oil then crush in the garlic and stir.

2. Wash the scallops in cold running water, then place them in the citrus and garlic marinade, cover and chill in the fridge for at least 1 hour.

3. Heat the oil in a frying pan and once hot, remove the scallops from the marinade and place them carefully in the pan. Cook on high heat for 1 minute on each side, until the scallops are sealed but still quite rare in the center. Try to keep them together in the pan, which should prevent them from stooping to one side.

4. Once cooked, remove the scallops from the heat and divide between 4 plates. Garnish with some chopped green onions, a few pieces of lemon rind and a drizzle of olive oil and season with salt and pepper.

COOK'S TIP

If you buy fresh scallops in their shells, after you have carefully removed the black sac, you can retain the scallop frills and the juices from inside the shell to make a delicious stock. Add them to a pan with 750 ml (3 cups) water, a chopped onion, a celery stick, 2 whole peeled garlic cloves and a bay leaf and simmer for 25 minutes.

Vegetable fritters

My sister Jo runs The Garlic Farm shop and restaurant. She's an inspired cook and a vegetarian. Cooking for the family is usually left in her hands these days, so we've all benefited from her ability to create wonderful vegetarian treats. She loves a good vegetable fritter and these two are my particular favorites.

Zucchini fritters

These are best made with fresh zucchini as they give off less water. If your grated zucchini seem watery, sprinkle them with salt and leave for 15 minutes. Then place them in a clean tea towel and wring out some of the liquid into the sink.

2 medium zucchinis, grated
250 ml (1 cup) mozzarella, grated
a handful of fresh mint leaves, finely chopped
2 garlic cloves
salt
freshly ground black pepper
50 ml (¼ cup) flour
30 ml (2 tablespoons) olive oil
sweet chili dipping sauce, to serve

Serves 4 as a starter

1. Place the grated zucchini, mozzarella and chopped mint into a large bowl. Crush in the garlic cloves, season with salt and freshly ground black pepper, then mix everything together.
2. Add in the flour and 15 ml (1 tablespoon) of olive oil and stir well until the ingredients start to bind. If the mixture seems too wet, add more flour. Shape the mixture into golf-ball-sized pieces, then flatten.
3. Heat the remaining olive oil in a non-stick frying pan over medium heat. Fry the fritters for 2–3 minutes on each side until golden brown.
4. Serve immediately with sweet chili dipping sauce.

Garlic, cumin and beet fritters

The brilliant color of these sweet and delicious mouthfuls make a wonderful starter to serve alongside freshly made tzatziki dip (see page 81) for dunking. Increase the quantities and pile them high for impressive party nibbles.

10 ml (2 teaspoons) cumin seeds

4 large raw beets, peeled and grated

50 ml (¼ cup) flour, plus extra for shaping fritters

2 garlic cloves

salt

freshly ground black pepper

45 ml (3 tablespoons) olive oil

tzatziki (page 81), to serve

Makes 12 small fritters

1. Heat a frying pan, add the cumin seeds and toast over high heat for 2 minutes to release their flavor.
2. In a bowl, combine the grated beets, flour and cumin seeds then crush in the garlic cloves and sprinkle with salt and pepper.
3. Use your hands to bring all the ingredients together, squeezing the mixture to absorb all the flour.
4. With wet hands, shape the mixture into small balls. (This can be a little awkward, but don't worry, the beets will hold their shape once in the oil.) Sprinkle some flour onto a plate and coat the balls in the flour.
5. Heat the olive oil in a non-stick frying pan over a medium heat. Carefully place the beet balls into the pan, fry on each side until crispy then place on paper towel to absorb excess oil.
6. Serve immediately with tzatziki dip.

COOK'S TIP

For a more formal dish, try serving these fritters on individual plates with tzatziki drizzled over the top. Accompany with a small watercress salad on the side. The flavors work perfectly, and, it looks beautiful too.

Braised red cabbage with garlic

This colorful side dish makes an excellent accompaniment to roast pork or game.

1 red cabbage, finely shredded
1 dessert apple, peeled, cored and chopped
   into small pieces
1 onion, halved and finely sliced
4 garlic cloves, crushed
45 ml (3 tablespoons) butter
5 ml (1 teaspoon) ground cinnamon
15 ml (1 tablespoon) soft brown sugar
45 ml (3 tablespoons) red wine vinegar
sea salt
freshly ground black pepper

Serves 6

1. Preheat the oven to 350°F.
2. Place all the ingredients into a large, closed ovenproof dish. Season and stir well, then bake in the oven for 1–1½ hours, stirring once or twice. Once cooked, the cabbage should be soft, not slushy.
3. Leave to cool then store in the fridge. It can be reheated in the oven or in a microwave.

Marinated minty garlic carrots ◗

Carrots can be made into a flavorful delight with this combination, which works well served alongside other tapas or as an accompaniment to cold cuts, especially lamb or beef. If you wish, you can prepare the dish ahead of time, adding the mint just before serving.

400 g (1 lb) carrots, peeled and sliced diagonally
4–5 garlic cloves, finely chopped
45 ml (3 tablespoons) apple cider vinegar
sea salt
freshly ground black pepper
a handful of mint leaves, finely chopped

Serves 4–6

1. Steam the carrots for about 5 minutes, until tender, then transfer to a serving bowl.
2. Toss with the garlic, vinegar and a good pinch of salt and pepper. Marinate for at least 15 minutes.
3. Add the mint, stir, and serve at room temperature or chilled.

Roasted garlic potatoes

Good roasted potatoes are to die for, and once you taste this simple variation, well, you might have to die twice!

1 kg (2 lbs) potatoes
50 ml (¼ cup) olive oil
salt
freshly ground black pepper
1 large garlic bulb, separated into unpeeled cloves
1 lemon, halved and squeezed
a few sprigs of rosemary, leaves only

Serves 4–6

1. Preheat the oven to 400°F.
2. Bring a large pan of salted water to a boil. Carefully add the potatoes and boil for around 7 minutes, or until they offer no resistance to a knife.
3. Drain the potatoes, then cut them in half and return to the pan. Holding a lid on the pan, shake the potatoes around to fluff up the edges. Now toss with the olive oil, salt and freshly ground black pepper, juice of the lemon and rosemary leaves.
4. Spread the potatoes in a roasting pan and distribute the garlic cloves among them. Add the lemon halves to the pan, then roast for 40 minutes, or until golden brown and crunchy. Discard the lemon halves before serving.

Garlic mashed potatoes

The inclusion of garlic in this dish gives a subtle, sweet flavor. It's great served with fish or roasted meats.

1 kg (2 lbs) potatoes, peeled and roughly chopped
1 garlic bulb, cloves peeled
2 bay leaves
500 ml (2 cups) milk
30 ml (2 tablespoons) butter
salt
freshly ground black pepper

Serves 4

1. Place the potatoes, garlic and bay leaves in a large saucepan then pour over the milk and enough water to cover the potatoes. Bring to a boil over a high heat then reduce the heat and simmer for 15 minutes, or until the potatoes are soft.
2. Drain the potatoes, retaining about one third of the cooking liquid, and discard the bay leaves.
3. Mash the potatoes and garlic well, adding 30 ml (2 tablespoons) of butter and drizzling in the cooking liquid until you reach the desired consistency. Season well with salt and freshly ground black pepper.
4. Serve immediately or keep warm in a covered large pan in a low oven.

Oak-smoked garlic dauphinoise

About a decade ago I lived in Paris for a few years, sharing an apartment with a lovely Canadian girl, Laura Calder, who was writing a cook book called *French Food at Home*. I had the pleasure of taste-testing many of her recipes, and when I gave her smoked garlic from the farm to try, she loved it so much that she added a recipe for smoked garlic dauphinoise in her book. Since it's hard to say whether or not smoked garlic has any health benefits, you can substitute it with ordinary garlic if you wish — it adds great flavor too.

1 kg (2 lbs) potatoes, thinly sliced

sea salt

freshly ground black pepper

5 ml (1 teaspoon) nutmeg, freshly grated

1 bulb oak-smoked garlic, cloves peeled (or 3–4 ordinary garlic cloves)

500 ml (2 cups) homogenized milk or milk mixed with cream

45 ml (3 tablespoons) butter, cut into slivers

Serves 4–6

1. Preheat the oven to 375°F.

2. Place half the sliced potatoes in a large ovenproof gratin dish. Cover with a layer of seasoning, then grate the garlic cloves over the top.

3. Tip the remainder of the potato slices into the dish, spreading them out evenly. Season again then pour in the milk and lay the butter slivers on top.

4. Bake in the oven until all the liquid has been absorbed and the top has browned, about 1–1½ hours.

5. Serve with roasted meat and green vegetables.

COOK'S TIP

This dish represents the ultimate comfort food. It's all about the long, slow cooking process so don't rush it. Check the dish halfway through and, if necessary, push the potatoes down so the cream is able to swim over and bubble on top. When it's ready, it should be really brown and crispy so make sure it's finished off to perfection.

Spicy sprouting broccoli

You can use this as a sauce served with noodles or as an accompaniment to grilled chicken.

600 g (1½ lb) sprouting broccoli or kale
5 ml (1 teaspoon) sesame seeds
7.5 ml (½ tablespoon) olive oil
7.5 ml (½ tablespoon) sesame oil
5 garlic cloves, finely sliced
a thumb-sized piece of ginger, finely sliced
1 red chili, deseeded and finely diced
15 ml (1 tablespoon) white wine vinegar
15 ml (1 tablespoon) light soy sauce

Serves 4

1. Bring a large pan of salted water to a boil. Add the broccoli and blanch for 3–4 minutes, then drain and set aside.
2. Meanwhile, heat a small frying pan, add the sesame seeds and toast over medium heat for 2 minutes until they start to pop. Set aside.
3. In another frying pan, heat the oils over medium heat, then add the garlic, ginger and chili, and fry gently for 2 minutes.
4. Add the broccoli and coat with the oil mixture. Add the vinegar and soy sauce and cook for a further 2 minutes.
5. Serve with the sesame seeds sprinkled over.

Salt and pepper squid with aioli

You can never make enough of this crunchy squid with aioli for dunking. It is very quick to prepare and makes an excellent starter.

aioli (see page 71)
4 squid, tubes and tentacles cleaned and sliced up
    1 cm (¼ in) thick
150 ml (¾ cup) plain flour
salt
freshly ground black pepper
5 ml (1 teaspoon) paprika
250 ml (1 cup) peanut or sunflower oil
1 lemon, cut into wedges

Serves 4

1. First, make the aioli – see recipe on page 71.
2. Heat the oil in a heavy-based pan until it reaches 350°F. If you don't have a thermometer, test the temperature by dropping a breadcrumb in the oil – it should turn golden brown in about a minute.
3. While the oil is heating, place the flour on a large plate, sprinkle in the paprika and season well. Toss the squid in the flour until it is completely coated. (Strain them in a sieve to remove any excess flour.)
4. Gently place the squid in the hot oil and fry for about 1–2 minutes, until golden. You may need to do this in batches – don't overfill the pan.
5. Use a slotted spoon to transfer the squid to a tray lined with paper towel. Serve with lemon wedges and the bowl of aïoli on the side.

Warm lentil and halloumi salad

My idea of heaven. Halloumi never fails to please in this quick and easy way to a delicious, healthy and filling lunch.

250 ml (1 cup) puy lentils

5 ml (1 teaspoon) vegetable bouillon powder

½ red onion, finely sliced

1 green chili, deseeded and finely sliced

30 ml (2 tablespoons) olive oil

2 garlic cloves

15 ml (1 tablespoon) olive oil

250 g (½ lb) halloumi, sliced

2 small zucchinis, cut into ribbons with a peeler

50 ml (¼ cup) pomegranate seeds

a handful of chopped fresh coriander, including stalks

sea salt

freshly ground black pepper

Serves 4

1. Cover the lentils with cold water and bring to a boil. Add the vegetable stock and cook for 15–20 minutes, or until the lentils are tender. Drain well.

2. While the lentils are still warm, place them in a large bowl. Add the onion, chili and olive oil then crush in the garlic cloves and stir well.

3. For the halloumi, heat the oil in a frying pan on medium heat. Add the halloumi and fry on each side until golden. Stir the zucchinis, pomegranate seeds and coriander into the bowl with the lentils. Season to taste.

4. Top the lentil mixture with the halloumi slices and serve.

COOK'S TIP

You can add garlic to almost any salad, either in a salad dressing or as very thin, lightly fried garlic slices, scattered over as a topping. Be careful not to burn the garlic, though, as this will make it taste bitter.

Som tam
Green papaya salad

Any visitor to Thailand will have come across this fantastic, fresh, hot and spicy dish made from green (unripe) papayas. It was my daily lunch when I lived in Bangkok, served by a street vendor from an enormous wooden bowl, which he used to pound all the ingredients together, like an oversized pestle and mortar. It's hard to replicate the exact flavors here but this combination comes quite close. Always use unripe papaya, never the ripe (orange) kind.

1 large green papaya, peeled, deseeded
  (or, if unavailable, 1 unripe mango, pit
  removed, or 1 cucumber, deseeded)
5 garlic cloves
3 red chilies, finely chopped (or to taste)
large pinch of salt
5 ml (1 teaspoon) dried shrimp or shrimp paste
15 ml (1 tablespoon) fish sauce
juice of 2 limes
15 ml (1 tablespoon) sugar
4 cherry tomatoes, cut into small slices
50 ml (¼ cup) beansprouts
50 ml (¼ cup) crushed peanuts

Serves 4

1. Shred the papaya (or mango or cucumber) into long, thin matchsticks.
2. Using a pestle and mortar, crush the garlic, chilies and salt. Add a small handful of the papaya and the dried shrimp or shrimp paste and gently pound until some of the juices are released.
3. Transfer to a bowl and stir in the rest of the ingredients, reserving some of the peanuts to sprinkle on top before serving.

COOK'S TIP

The raw freshness of this dish not only gives a beautiful crunchy texture and delicious flavors but also makes it very nutritious. Surprisingly filling and very easy to prepare, it makes a great light lunch alternative to your average sandwich.

Chicken with 40 garlic cloves

Happily, some 1970s dinner-party classics are making a comeback, including this traditional French dish, which makes the most of garlic's sweet, rich flavor by cooking the cloves encased in their skins. Once cooked, the cloves can be served as they are, so that guests can squeeze garlic onto their plates. Alternatively, use the extracted flesh to create a deliciously creamy sauce.

2 celery stalks, chopped

1 large organic chicken (about 1.6 kg/3.5 lb)

2 large sprigs of rosemary

2 large sprigs of thyme

3–4 large garlic bulbs

30 ml (2 tablespoons) olive oil

salt

freshly ground black pepper

2 bay leaves

1 large carrot, diced

1 small onion, cut into wedges

2 large glasses of red cooking wine

Serves 4–6

1. Preheat the oven to 375°F.

2. Place the chopped celery, 1 sprig of each herb and a handful of unpeeled garlic cloves into the chicken cavity.

3. Place half the remaining cloves in a lidded casserole, put the chicken on top, brush with olive oil and season well. Arrange the bay leaves, carrot, onion and remaining herbs and garlic cloves around the chicken.

4. Drizzle with olive oil then pour over the red wine. Cover and roast for at least 1 hour 20 minutes, or until the chicken is tender and the juices run clear when the flesh is pierced with a skewer.

5. Either serve with toasted bread, spread with the soft flesh of the garlic cloves, or blend the garlic flesh with the juices from the bottom of the casserole to make a creamy sauce.

Spaghetti carbonara

Pasta sauces lend themselves particularly well to the addition of garlic. There are several ways of preparing this Italian favorite, but my recipe includes using extra garlic for enhanced flavor and health benefits.

1 tablespoon olive oil

6 thick slices of pancetta or bacon, chopped into small pieces

4 shallots, finely diced

4 fat garlic cloves, finely chopped

4 large free-range eggs

125 ml (½ cup) Parmesan, freshly grated

freshly ground black pepper

500 g (1 lb) fresh spaghetti

2 green onions, chopped

a handful of fresh basil leaves, chopped

a handful of fresh parsley leaves, chopped

Serves 4

1. Heat the oil in a large frying pan on medium heat and gently fry the pancetta, shallots and garlic for 5–7 minutes, or until the shallots have softened.
2. In a bowl, lightly beat the eggs and most of the grated Parmesan, reserving a little for the garnish. Season with freshly ground black pepper.
3. Boil the pasta in a large pan of salted boiling water according to packet instructions, about 2–3 minutes.
4. Drain the cooked spaghetti, then return it to the pan, off the heat. Quickly add the pancetta, shallots and garlic and pour in the egg mixture, stirring well.
5. Add the green onions, basil and parsley, and stir well again.
6. Serve immediately, sprinkled with freshly ground black pepper and extra Parmesan.

COOK'S TIP

When sautéing garlic, make sure it never turns more than pale gold to light brown in color and never allow it to turn dark brown as this will impair the flavor. If you wish to keep the garlic flavors subtle, it is best to lightly sauté the garlic briefly in oil then, before it turns brown, allow it to simmer with the juices of the other ingredients.

Garlic mushroom pizza

Home-made pizza is as satisfying to prepare as it is to eat. This recipe is a recreation of a mouth-watering pizza I was served in Verona. It has no tomato sauce, which means it's even quicker to make — and you'll be surprised that you don't even miss it. Serve with mixed greens.

For the base:

480 g (4 cups) plain flour, plus extra for dusting

1 packet (6 g) dried yeast

30 ml (2 tablespoons) olive oil

10 ml (2 teaspoons) sugar or honey

For the topping:

300 g (¾ lb) porcini or other flavorful mushrooms, sliced

a few sprigs of fresh rosemary, finely chopped

4 garlic cloves, peeled

olive oil

salt and freshly ground black pepper

250 ml (1 cup) buffalo mozzarella, chopped

50 ml (¼ cup) grated Parmesan

Makes 2 large pizzas

1. To make the base, mix the flour and yeast in a large bowl and make a well in the center. In a jug, mix the olive oil and sugar or honey with 300 ml (1¼ cup) warm water, then pour into the well of the flour mixture and gradually mix to form a soft and slightly sticky dough.

2. Transfer the dough to a lightly floured work surface and lightly flour your hands. Knead the dough by hand for at least 10 minutes, until smooth and pliable. Place the dough back in the bowl and cover with oiled plastic wrap. Leave to rise for 45 minutes or until doubled in size.

3. Preheat the oven to 400°F.

4. Place the mushrooms and chopped rosemary sprigs into a bowl. Crush in the garlic, pour in 2–3 tablespoons of olive oil, season with salt and freshly ground pepper and combine well.

5. Remove the plastic wrap from the dough and divide it into two balls. On a lightly floured work surface, carefully stretch them out into round bases about ½ cm (¼ inch) thick.

6. Cover each base with the mushroom mixture then top with mozzarella and Parmesan.

7. Bake the pizzas in the oven until the bases are crisp and golden-brown around the edges and the cheese has melted.

Roasted butternut squash and garlic risotto

As well as being sweet and delicious, butternut squash is packed with vitamins and minerals, adding an extra health kick to this vegetarian dinner.

1 large butternut squash, cut into large chunks, seeds removed
3–4 large garlic cloves, peeled
15 ml (1 tablespoon) olive oil, plus extra for drizzling
a few sprigs of thyme, plus 1 tablespoon chopped thyme
salt
freshly ground black pepper
50 ml (¼ cup) butter
1 large onion, finely chopped
250 ml (1 cup) risotto rice
125 ml (½ cup) white wine
1 L (4 cups) vegetable stock
a handful of freshly grated Parmesan, plus extra to serve
a handful of toasted pine nuts, to serve

Serves 4

1. Preheat the oven to 375°F.
2. Place the butternut squash in a large bowl then crush in 1–2 garlic cloves, drizzle with olive oil, throw in the thyme sprigs and season well. Mix thoroughly, making sure the squash gets a good covering of oil and the garlic is well distributed.
3. Put the mixture on a large roasting pan and roast in the oven for 30–40 minutes, or until the edges of the squash begin to brown.
4. Remove the squash from the oven and allow it to cool slightly before scraping the flesh away from the skin into a bowl, removing any thyme twigs. Scrape any sticky juices left in the tray into the bowl and mash the squash. Keep warm while making the risotto.
5. Heat the olive oil and 30 ml (2 tablespoons) butter in a heavy-based saucepan or sauté pan, then add the onion and gently fry until softened, about 2 minutes. Crush in 2 garlic cloves and gently fry for a further 2 minutes. Add the rice and stir well so the grains become coated in the butter and oil. Pour in the wine and stir well until absorbed. Add a ladleful of hot stock and stir until absorbed. Keep the pan simmering while gradually adding more stock and continuing to stir, until the rice is cooked al dente, about 15–20 minutes. The risotto should have a smooth and creamy consistency. Add more stock if necessary.
6. Remove from the heat and add the mashed squash, 30 ml (2 tablespoons) butter, grated Parmesan, 1 tablespoon chopped thyme and seasoning to taste. Stir well.
7. Serve with a topping of toasted pine nuts and a sprinkling of grated or shaved Parmesan.

Asian fish parcel

A magical trio of flavors –
chili, garlic and ginger – works
particularly well in this quick and
simple fish dinner, which can be
made using fresh or frozen fish.

olive oil

4 large fillets of pollack, or other sustainable white fish

a thumb-sized piece of ginger, peeled and grated

8 garlic cloves, sliced

2 red chilies, finely sliced

50 ml (¼ cup) light soy sauce

7.5 ml (½ tablespoon) toasted sesame oil

2 bok choy, finely sliced

2 green onions, finely chopped, to garnish

a handful of fresh coriander, roughly chopped, to garnish

250 ml (1 cup) steamed jasmine rice, to serve

Serves 4

1. Preheat the oven to 350°F.
2. Take 4 sheets of aluminum foil, large enough to
loosely encase each fillet, and lay on a work surface.
Brush one side of each sheet with olive oil.
3. Place a fish fillet in the center of each sheet then
arrange on a baking tray, bringing the sides of the
sheets up around the fish.
4. Top each fillet with the ginger, garlic, chili and soy
sauce, then fold over the foil to seal. Transfer the tray
to the oven and bake the parcels for 15–20 minutes.
In the meantime, lightly sauté the bok choy in sesame
oil for 3–4 minutes on medium heat.
5. Serve the fish on a bed of jasmine rice alongside
the bok choy with the juices from the parcels and
garnished with chopped coriander and green onions.

Spicy beef, garlic and scapes stir-fry

Garlic scapes bring a fantastic
crunchy texture with fresh garlic
flavors to all sorts of dishes.

30 ml (2 tablespoons) light soy sauce

a thumb-sized piece of ginger, peeled and grated

1 small red chili

5 ml (1 teaspoon) sesame oil

2 large garlic cloves

500 g (1 lb) sirloin steak, cut into thin strips

250 ml (1 cup) garlic scapes (or green onions or garlic
    chives), 6 cm (2 in) long

30 ml (2 tablespoons) sunflower oil

1 red pepper, sliced

50 ml (¼ cup) hot beef stock

250 ml (1 cup) steamed white rice, to serve

Serves 4

1. Combine the soy sauce, ginger, chili and sesame
oil in a bowl. Crush in the garlic and add the steak,
tossing to coat it completely. Let it stand for
15 minutes.
2. Blanch the scapes for 2 minutes in salted boiling
water, then drain and set aside.
3. Heat the oil in a wok and, on high heat, fry the
steak strips in 2 batches for about 2 minutes each. The
meat should be browned on the outside but still pink
in the middle. Heat the rest of the oil in the wok, add
the red pepper and fry for a minute or so, then add
the scapes, all the steak, any remaining juices from the
marinade and the stock and stir-fry until piping hot.
Serve immediately on plain rice.

Barbecued garlic and lime snapper

This dish is inspired by visits to Sydney, where the freshness and abundance of seafood means that the fish I consider to be a treat are casually served at backyard barbecues. With the strong Asian influences in Australian cuisine, garlic often features heavily. This whole fish can be cooked on a barbecue or baked in the oven.

1.5 kg (3 lbs) whole snapper or other whole large fish

1 stick of lemongrass, trimmed, halved and cut
    5 cm (2 in) long

6 garlic cloves, peeled and bashed

6 Asian lime leaves, torn

sea salt

freshly ground black pepper

a handful of fresh coriander

2 green onions, finely sliced

2 limes

250 ml (1 cup) steamed white rice, to serve

For the dressing:

50 ml (3 tablespoons) sweet chili sauce

juice of 2 limes

5 ml (1 teaspoon) brown sugar

45 ml (3 tablespoon) light soy sauce

1 small thumb-length of ginger, peeled and finely grated

2 garlic cloves, crushed

15 ml (1 tablespoon) fish sauce

30 ml (2 tablespoons) peanut oil

Serves 6

1. Light the barbecue or preheat the oven to 375°F.

2. Wash the fish under running water and pat dry with paper towel. Using a sharp knife, slash the fish with about 3 cuts 1 cm (a ¼ in) deep across the fattest part, then place the whole fish on a large sheet of aluminum foil, enough to be able to enclose it loosely. Fill the cavity of the fish with the lemongrass, garlic and lime leaves. Season well with sea salt and freshly ground black pepper, then enclose the fish loosely in the foil.

3. Place the fish on the barbecue or in the oven for about 30–40 minutes, turning it halfway through. In the meantime, you can make the dressing by combining all the ingredients in a small jar or gravy boat.

4. Unwrap the fish and check that it is cooked through, then transfer onto a serving plate. Pour the dressing over the fish and sprinkle the coriander and green onions on top. Serve with lime wedges and plain rice.

Brazilian fish stew - *Moqueca*

As one Brazilian restaurant owner put it to me, "Brazilians love garlic the way Mexicans love chili." Combine the national love of garlic with a 4,655-mile coastline and it's clear why *Moqueca* has been a national dish there for over 300 years. While you may not have fresh Brazilian fish on your doorstep, any meaty, firm fish will work well in this tropical stew; just make sure it's from a sustainable source.

1 medium onion, chopped

a thumb-sized piece of ginger, peeled and finely chopped

6 large garlic cloves, peeled

3 plum tomatoes, deseeded and chopped

juice of 2 limes

sea salt

freshly ground black pepper

4 white sustainably sourced fish fillets, chopped into large chunks

50 ml (3 tablespoons) palm oil or olive oil

1 green pepper, deseeded and chopped

1 yellow pepper, deseeded and chopped

15 ml (1 tablespoon) tomato purée

1 bay leaf

400 ml (1¾ cups) fish stock

400 ml (1¾ cups) coconut milk

juice of ½ lemon

a handful of fresh parsley

250 ml (1 cup) steamed white rice

Serves 4

1. Place half the onion, ginger and garlic in a blender along with one of the chopped tomatoes and all the lime juice. Season well with salt and pepper and blend until smooth.

2. Place the fish in a bowl and pour the marinade directly over them, turning the fish to coat it completely, then cover with plastic wrap and chill in the fridge for at least 2 hours.

3. Heat the oil in a heavy-based pan and, when hot, add the remaining onion, green and yellow peppers and cook to soften for a few minutes. Add the tomato purée and remaining ginger to the pan, crush in the remaining garlic and cook for another couple of minutes. Then add the remaining chopped tomatoes, bay leaf and fish stock, bring to a boil and simmer for 10 minutes.

4. Add the coconut milk and bring to a boil before carefully adding the fish mixture you prepared earlier. Cook for about 3 minutes or until the fish is cooked through. Add lemon juice and salt and pepper to taste.

5. Distribute the stew into 4 bowls and sprinkle each with a pinch of chopped fresh parsley. Serve with white rice.

Slow roasted lamb with mint yogurt sauce

Don't be put off by the long cooking time for this dish. It's incredibly quick and easy to prepare, and slow roasting allows the meat to become tender as well as giving fantastic flavor. You can leave it to cook overnight or prepare it in the morning for supper.

2 kg (4 lb) shoulder of lamb
salt
freshly ground black pepper
30 ml (2 tablespoons) olive oil
3 onions, sliced
4 carrots, quartered lengthwise
1 garlic bulb or 8–10 cloves, peeled but left whole
1 bay leaf
250 ml (1 cup) white wine
250 ml (1 cup) vegetable, beef or chicken stock

For the sauce:
45 ml (3 tablespoons) plain yogurt
2 sprigs of fresh mint, leaves only
salt
pepper

Serves 4–6

1. Preheat the oven to 250°F.
2. Season the lamb well with salt and freshly ground black pepper.
3. Heat the olive oil in a large roasting pot on high heat. Add the lamb joint to the roasting pot and fry for about 15 minutes, turning regularly, until browned all over. Turn down the heat.
4. Add the vegetables, garlic cloves and bay leaf around the meat, then pour in the wine and stock. Bring to a boil before placing the casserole in the oven. Cook for up to 7 hours. (Although the meat will be cooked after about 5 hours, it's best left for the full time if possible.) Turn the meat halfway through cooking.
5. Remove the pot from the oven and transfer the lamb and vegetables to a serving dish. Cover with aluminum foil and return to the oven to keep warm.
6. To make the sauce, skim off any excess fat from the liquid in the pot and place the pot on the stove top on medium heat. Boil until the liquid has reduced by about a quarter, then add the yogurt and mint leaves, stirring well. Reduce the heat so the sauce comes to a simmer, remove the mint leaves and add seasoning if needed.
7. Pour the sauce into a gravy pot and serve the lamb with mashed potatoes and a steamed green vegetable.

Roast garlic chicken

Nothing beats the enticing aroma of roast chicken and garlic. By smearing garlic herb butter under the chicken skin, you'll get the garlic flavors into the meat too.

2 garlic bulbs

45 ml (3 tablespoons) butter, softened

3–4 sprigs of rosemary

3–4 large sprigs of thyme

1 lemon

salt

black pepper

1 large organic chicken (about 1.6 kg/3 lbs)

6 ripe tomatoes, halved

3 onions, quartered

olive oil

Serves 4–6

1. Preheat the oven to 400°F.

2. First make the garlic herb butter. Remove 2 cloves from the garlic bulbs, peel and then crush them in a bowl with the butter, 2 chopped rosemary and thyme sprigs and the zest of half the lemon. Season with salt and black pepper and mix well.

3. Cut the lemon into halves and place them in the cavity of the chicken along with the onions and half the remaining herbs.

4. Starting at the neck end of the bird, gently push your fingers under the skin and spread the garlic herb butter evenly. If you wish, you can do the same with the legs by making a small slit in the skin and pushing the butter underneath.

5. Place the chicken in a large roasting dish, rub all over with olive oil and season with salt and black pepper. Roast for 45 minutes.

6. Remove the chicken from the oven. Cut the garlic bulbs in half horizontally then arrange them around the chicken together with the tomatoes and onions, and drizzle over olive oil. Reduce the oven temperature to 320°F then continue to roast the chicken for 45 minutes, covering it with aluminum foil if it starts to brown too quickly.

7. Test that the chicken is cooked by inserting a skewer into the thickest part of the meat – the juices should run clear.

8. To serve, place a garlic half on each plate – the roasted flesh can be satisfyingly squeezed out of its skin – and accompany with green vegetables and potatoes.

Spicy chickpea curry

Not all curries include vast quantities of garlic, but many certainly benefit from the great base flavors it creates. Frying crushed garlic and ginger together is one of my favorite ways to start a curry dish. This one is delicious, healthy and economical, and I always find it tastes even better the day after I've made it.

30 ml (2 tablespoons) olive oil

1 onion, finely chopped

6 garlic cloves, crushed

a thumb-sized piece of ginger, grated

2 red chilies, deseeded and finely chopped

5 ml (1 teaspoon) turmeric

5 ml (1 teaspoon) ground cumin

10 ml (2 teaspoons) ground coriander

5 ml (1 teaspoon) garam masala

500 ml (2 cups) canned chickpeas

400 g (1 lb) canned chopped tomatoes

75 ml (⅓ cup) red lentils

125 ml (½ cup) coconut cream

1 head of broccoli, chopped into small florets

sea salt

freshly ground black pepper

2 handfuls of fresh coriander, chopped, to garnish

250 ml (1 cup) brown rice, cooked

Serves 4

1. Heat the olive oil in a deep saucepan or a wok and fry the onion, garlic, ginger and chilies on a medium heat for 2 minutes.

2. Add the spices and fry for a further 5 minutes, adding more oil if necessary.

3. Pour in the chickpeas and tomatoes, add the lentils and coconut cream then simmer until the lentils have softened.

4. Add the broccoli and simmer for a further 5 minutes then season to taste.

5. Garnish with a sprinkling of coriander and serve with the brown rice.

COOK'S TIP

Pairing ginger and garlic is one of the building blocks of Indian cuisine and ginger-garlic paste is an indispensable ingredient in many condiments and curries. You make it with equal quantities of garlic and ginger, blended together, and Indian cooks often make up huge batches as it's something they can guarantee they'll be using every day.

Tandoori chicken

This delicious Indian dish wouldn't be the same without garlic adding heat to the spicy yogurt marinade.

8 chicken thighs, drumsticks or 4 breasts, skinned

pinch of salt

juice of 1 lemon

a thumb-sized piece of ginger, peeled and grated

6 garlic cloves, crushed

2 green chilies, finely chopped

10 ml (2 teaspoons) garam masala

10 ml (2 teaspoons) sumac

50 ml (¼ cup) plain Greek yogurt

30 ml (2 tablespoons) butter

To serve:

juice of 1 lemon

1 red onion, finely sliced

salt and freshly ground black pepper

2 handfuls of fresh mint leaves

50 ml (¼ cup) plain Greek yogurt

flatbread

Serves 4

1. Cut a few incisions into the chicken pieces using a small, sharp knife. Place the chicken into a bowl then sprinkle over the salt, lemon juice and all the spices, massaging into the chicken until well coated.

2. Add 50 ml (¼ cup) of yogurt and mix with the chicken and spices. Cover and refrigerate overnight or for a minimum of 4 hours.

3. Preheat the oven to its highest setting.

4. Remove the chicken pieces from the yogurt and lay them in a roasting pan or on a baking tray, making sure they have plenty of room. Roast in the center of the oven for 20 minutes. Halfway through cooking, add a knob of butter on top of the chicken to give it a nice browned finish.

5. Remove the chicken from the oven and leave to rest for 5 minutes.

6. To serve, squeeze the lemon juice over the onion slices and season. Pile the dressed onion and mint leaves onto a plate with the tandoori chicken and accompany with yogurt and flatbread on the side.

Aioli

This extremely versatile garlic mayonnaise is originally from the Provence region in the south of France, which helps explain the origin of the name. *Ail* is the French word for garlic and "oli" is from the Latin *oleum*, meaning oil. It works equally well served as a dip with steamed vegetables or as a sauce to accompany fish or meat.

3 large garlic cloves, peeled
2 free-range egg yolks
15 ml (1 tablespoon) Dijon mustard
300 ml (1 cup) olive oil
juice of ¼ lemon
salt
freshly ground black pepper

1. Using a pestle and mortar, crush the garlic with a pinch of salt to form a paste.
2. In a bowl, whisk the garlic, egg yolks and mustard together.
3. Add the olive oil in a steady pour and whisk until all the oil is absorbed and the mixture has thickened.
4. Add the lemon juice and season to taste. If you'd like to use the aioli as a sauce, whisk in a few drops of warm water to make it runnier.

The Garlic Farm classic hummus

We serve this hummus in The Garlic Farm café, and the bowl is always returned as if it's been licked clean. Need I say more?

500 ml (2 cups) canned chickpeas, drained
juice of ½ lemon
5 ml (1 teaspoon) cumin
3 garlic cloves, peeled and crushed
15 ml (1 tablespoon) chopped coriander
10 ml (2 teaspoons) tahini
30–45 ml (2–3 tablespoons) olive oil
large pinch of salt
cracked black pepper

Place all the ingredients in a food processor and blend. To keep a thicker texture, don't blend for too long. Serve with any combination of raw vegetables, breadsticks or warmed pita bread.

The best whole roasted garlic

We've tried and tested so many different ways of roasting garlic at home and in our farm café. After much deliberation, this is our recommended method for the most succulent, juicy, sweet cloves. You can serve the whole bulb alongside roasted meats.

1 whole garlic bulb per person
olive oil

1. Preheat the oven to 350°F.
2. Cover the outside of the bulb(s) in olive oil. Loosely wrap them in aluminum foil (you can use a roasting pot if you have one) then roast in the oven for 1 hour.
3. Unwrap the aluminum foil or remove the lid of the roasting pot and roast uncovered for a further 10 minutes.
4. To serve, slice the bulb horizontally, making a kind of lid that can be lifted up to spoon out the soft flesh of the cloves.

Cucumber kimchi ◖

The Koreans have been eating this incredibly healthy dish with almost every meal for centuries, the earliest references to Kimchi being from at least 2,600 years ago. It is made with fermented vegetables, usually cabbage, combined with many flavors and spices, including garlic. Here is a cucumber-based version which is relatively easy to prepare and the crispy crunch of the cucumber combined with garlic and chili taste delicious.

700 g (1½ lbs) small cucumbers (pickling cucumbers work best but large cucumbers also work)

30 ml (2 tablespoons) sea salt

½ onion, finely chopped

4 green onions, sliced lengthwise then chopped on the diagonal

4 garlic cloves

1 small red chili, deseeded and finely chopped (optional)

15–30 ml (1–2 tablespoons) Korean chili pepper powder, *gochugaru* (or any red chili powder)

10 ml (2 teaspoons) honey

10 ml (2 teaspoons) vinegar

Makes 1 large batch, enough for 2 large jars

1. Wash and chop the cucumbers into 3 cm (2 in) long pieces.
2. Place them in a large ceramic bowl and sprinkle with the salt, then leave at room temperature overnight or at least for a few hours.
3. Add the onion and green onions to the cucumber, crush in the garlic cloves and then add the chili, chili powder, honey and vinegar. Mix all the ingredients together well.
4. Place the mixture in the fridge to cool. When cooled, you can eat this right away or, alternatively, transfer into 2 large sterilized jars, and leave it to ferment at room temperature for a couple of days before putting it in the fridge. As the cucumbers will eventually lose their crunch, it is best to eat this kimchi within a week or so.

HEALTH BENEFITS

The beauty of this side dish or *banchan*, as the Koreans call it, is that it not only livens up your palate but is also the key to maintaining a healthy digestive system thanks to the presence of gut-friendly bacteria, lactobacillus. Western diets typically lack fermented foods and many would argue that this is of great detriment to our health.

Pickled garlic with lemons and limes

Delicious homemade pickles have long been a favorite in our family, which is why we make and sell a huge range of pickles and chutneys at The Garlic Farm. And as we're constantly coming up with new creations, our range is growing by the year. This is a recipe we haven't yet made available in the farm shop, though I'm sure you'll see it on the shelves sooner or later as it's a real winner. I've chosen to share it in this book because it's very easy to make at home, unlike some of our recipes that require a long list of ingredients and much more preparation time.

30 ml (3 tablespoons) mustard seeds
10 ml (1 tablespoon) fenugreek seeds
30 ml (2 tablespoons) peanut oil for frying
5 ml (1 teaspoon) turmeric
10 ml (1 tablespoon) red chili powder
3 unwaxed lemons, cut into small chunks
3 unwaxed limes, cut into small chunks
   (rinds on, seeds discarded)
2 garlic bulbs, cloves peeled
45 ml (3 tablespoons) sea salt

1. Using a pestle and mortar, crush the mustard and fenugreek seeds.
2. Heat the oil in a pan and gently fry all the spices for 2 minutes, then add the fruit, garlic cloves and salt, stir and remove from the heat.
3. Place the mixture in an airtight container or jar. Try to choose a container that doesn't leave too much air when filled with the mixture.
4. Leave to ripen in the fridge for at least 10 days, turning occasionally.

Pesto ♦

This classic pesto recipe and variation offer a simple yet delicious way of introducing more garlic into your diet – I'm always generous with the garlic, so you may vary the quantities to suit your taste. The sauce can be stirred into freshly cooked pasta, added to sandwiches or bruschetta, mixed into bean salads, spread over roasted meats or used as stuffing for chicken breasts.

Classic pesto

30 ml (2 tablespoons) pine nuts
large bunch of fresh basil leaves
2 large garlic cloves, peeled
125 ml (½ cup) olive oil
juice of ¼ lemon
30 ml (2 tablespoons) Parmesan, grated
sea salt to taste

1. Lightly toast the pine nuts in a frying pan, until they are pale golden brown.
2. Put the toasted pine nuts and remaining ingredients, except the Parmesan, in a food processor and pulse until the desired consistency is reached – I prefer pesto to have a little texture.
3. Stir in the grated Parmesan and add salt to taste.

Green garlic pesto

3 large green garlic bulbs, roots removed
2 garlic cloves, peeled and chopped
50 ml (¼ cup) olive oil
5 ml (1 teaspoon) salt
50 ml (¼ cup) mixed seeds (pine nuts, pumpkin seeds and sunflower seeds)
a good handful of fresh basil leaves
400 ml (1¾ cups) Parmesan or pecorino, finely grated
sea salt to taste

1. Finely chop the bulbs, stems and leaves.
2. Place all the ingredients, except the cheese, in a food processor and pulse until you reach the desired consistency.
3. Stir in the cheese and add salt to taste. Mix in more olive oil if the pesto is too dry.

EARLY HARVEST

If you can't wait for the garlic harvest in July, this is the perfect way to enjoy an early crop. As green garlic usually has lower allicin levels than matured garlic, I suggest adding a couple of cloves to boost the health benefits.

Classic vinaigrette 🧄

The use of sunflower oil instead of olive oil makes this dressing much lighter, making it the perfect partner for a crunchy green salad.

30 ml (2 tablespoons) white wine vinegar
50 ml (¼ cup) sunflower oil
5 ml (1 teaspoon) Dijon mustard
1 garlic clove, peeled and crushed
sea salt
freshly ground black pepper

Put the vinegar, oil, mustard and garlic in a screw-top jar and season. Cover the jar and shake well to combine. Store in a cool place until ready to use, adding fresh herbs just before serving if desired. Freshly made vinaigrette will keep in a jar for up to a week, or in a sealed container in the fridge for several weeks.

Garlic and coriander yogurt dressing 🧄

50 ml (¼ cup) plain yogurt
juice of ¼ lemon
a piece of ginger 3 cm (¼ in), peeled and grated
1 garlic clove, peeled and crushed
handful of fresh coriander, roughly chopped

Mix all the ingredients together in a bowl.

Moroccan dressing 🧄

125 ml (½ cup) extra virgin olive oil
45 ml (3 tablespoons) red wine vinegar
5 ml (1 teaspoon) sweet paprika
2.5 ml (½ teaspoon) ground cumin
1 garlic clove, finely chopped
handful of fresh flat-leaf parsley, finely chopped

Mix all the ingredients together in a bowl.

Salsa verde ♠

Served with grilled or roasted meat and fish, drizzled over a bean salad or stirred through pasta, this sauce is always a sensation. You can double the quantities and refrigerate for up to 3 days or freeze for up to 2 months.

3 garlic cloves, peeled
10 ml (2 teaspoons) Dijon mustard
2 small gherkins
4 anchovy fillets
small bunch of fresh flat-leaf parsley
small bunch of fresh mint leaves
small bunch of fresh basil leaves
250 ml (1 cup) extra virgin olive oil
juice and zest of 1 lemon
salt & freshly ground pepper to taste

Place all the ingredients in a blender and blend until smooth. Add extra seasoning if necessary.

COOK'S TIP

Both children and adults will love its sweet, rich flavor, and conveniently it can be kept in the fridge for a few weeks. Use it as a dip, on baked potatoes, spread on toast, stirred through pasta or as a condiment for grilled meats.

Garlic spread

Some people find garlic's heat a little too much for their taste buds. This Provençal-style recipe is a brilliant way to create a gentle and versatile garlic paste.

1–2 garlic bulbs, cloves peeled
500 ml (2 cups) milk
250 ml (1 cup) olive oil
seasoning and herbs

1. Place the cloves in a heavy-based saucepan and pour over enough milk to just cover them. Bring to a boil, then drain the cloves and rinse them in cold water.
2. Return the cloves to the pan and repeat with fresh milk. Do this 3–4 times, using fresh milk each time. The stronger the garlic, the more boiling is required.
3. Finally, drain the cloves, rinse them in cold water then pat them dry with paper towel. Place the cloves back in the pan and cover with olive oil. Keep on low heat for 1 hour – the temperature must not exceed 150°F.
4. Either store the sweet cloves in the oil in the fridge or mash them with some seasoning and your choice of herbs to make a paste.

Hot tomato salsa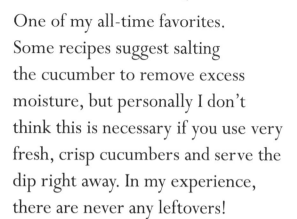

One of our best-selling Garlic Farm relishes is a very hot tomato and garlic salsa called Vampire Relish. This is a variation that uses fresh tomatoes and will definitely ensure no fanged friends dare come to your party.

4 large vine-ripened tomatoes, roughly chopped
½ red onion, roughly chopped
2 garlic cloves, peeled and chopped
juice of 1 lime
10 ml (2 teaspoons) dried chili flakes
10 ml (2 teaspoons) chili sauce (e.g. Tabasco), or to taste
15 ml (1 tablespoon) red wine vinegar
salt and freshly ground black pepper to taste
a few sprigs of fresh parsley, finely chopped

1. Place all the ingredients, except the parsley, in a food processor. Blend carefully to keep the mixture slightly chunky.
2. Stir in the parsley, season to taste and refrigerate until needed. It tastes better if left for a couple of hours before serving with tortilla chips.

Tzatziki

One of my all-time favorites. Some recipes suggest salting the cucumber to remove excess moisture, but personally I don't think this is necessary if you use very fresh, crisp cucumbers and serve the dip right away. In my experience, there are never any leftovers!

250 ml (1 cup) thick Greek yogurt
125 ml (½ cup) crème fraîche or sour cream
½ large cucumber, peeled, deseeded and finely diced
2 garlic cloves, peeled and crushed
15 ml (1 tablespoon) finely chopped fresh parsley
15 ml (1 tablespoon) finely chopped fresh mint, plus extra to garnish
15 ml (1 tablespoon) olive oil
juice of ¼ lemon
salt and freshly ground black pepper

Simply stir all the ingredients together, adjusting the seasoning if necessary, then spoon into a serving bowl and garnish with a sprinkle of chopped mint. Serve as an appetiser or snack with crudités (batons of raw carrot, celery, etc.), toasted pita bread or chips. Alternatively, tzatziki makes a refreshing side to sizzling lamb chops.

Garlic and rosemary focaccia

Including garlic in bread dough itself, I found out the hard way, can impair the dough's ability to rise. This recipe avoids this pitfall by adding the garlic as a topping instead. Focaccia is very easy to make and is always popular with the whole family. My children devour it.

750 ml (3 cups) flour, plus extra for dusting

7 g (¼ oz) packet fast action yeast

5 ml (1 teaspoon) salt

400 ml (1¾ cup) warm water

(5–10 ml) 1–2 teaspoons honey or sugar

50 ml (¼ cup) olive oil, plus extra for oiling

4 garlic cloves

3 sprigs of fresh rosemary, leaves only, finely chopped

sea salt

Makes 1 large or 2 medium-sized loaves

1. Place the flour, yeast and 5 ml (1 teaspoon) salt in a large bowl and make a well in the middle.

2. Fill a measuring jug with just over 300 ml (1¼ cup) warm water and stir in the honey or sugar and olive oil. Pour most of this mixture into the bowl of flour, stirring with a wooden spoon or your fingers to bring the dough together. Add a little more water if necessary until the dough has a soft, slightly wet consistency that is easily workable.

3. Place the dough on a lightly floured work surface and knead for at least 10 minutes, until it becomes elastic and smooth.

4. Clean, dry and oil the bowl before placing the dough back in, then cover with oiled plastic wrap. Leave to rise in a warm place until it has doubled in size.

5. Preheat the oven to 375°F.

6. Once the dough has risen, knock it back on a clean floured work surface. Shape the dough into one or two oval-shaped flat loaves, transfer onto baking pans then leave to rise again for about 20 minutes.

7. In the meantime, pour 30 ml (2 tablespoons) olive oil into a small bowl, crush in the garlic cloves, stir in the chopped rosemary and mix well.

8. When the dough has risen, make holes in it with your fingertips then pour over the garlic and rosemary mixture, making sure it gets into the holes.

9. Sprinkle with plenty of sea salt and place in the oven to bake for 30 minutes, or until golden and hollow-sounding when tapped on the bottom.

10. Turn out onto a wire rack to cool.

The very best cheesy garlic bread

Garlic and bread can be combined in a huge variety of ways. We've tried many at the farm and can guarantee this one will be polished off quickly.

125 ml (½ cup) butter
3–4 large garlic cloves
250 ml (1 cup) mozzarella
250 ml (1 cup) cheddar
a handful of fresh herbs – parsley, basil and oregano all work well
1 fresh baguette, sliced diagonally at 4–5 cm (1–2 in) intervals
paprika for sprinkling

1. Preheat the oven to 375°F.
2. Put all the filling ingredients in a blender or food processor and blend.
3. Generously spread the filling between the baguette slices. Wrap the baguette loosely in aluminum foil, then place in the oven for 20–25 minutes, until the filling has melted.
4. Remove from the oven, open the foil and sprinkle with paprika. Leaving the foil open, return the baguette to the oven for a few minutes, until the crust is golden brown.

The Garlic Farm toasted ciabatta

At The Garlic Farm café, our talented chef, Charlie, likes to use the different varieties of garlic we grow to suit different dishes. He recommends strong-flavored Chesnok Wight for this garlic bread.

125 ml (½ cup) salted butter, softened
3 fat Chesnok Wight cloves, or other strong-flavored garlic variety, finely chopped
1 sprig of fresh rosemary, leaves only, finely chopped
2 ciabatta loaves, cut lengthwise
chili flakes, optional

1. Mix the butter with the garlic and rosemary.
2. Spread the ciabatta with a thick layer of garlic butter. Place on a grill tray and grill until golden brown.
3. Cut the toasted ciabatta diagonally and serve. Add a light sprinkling of chili flakes to spice it up if you wish.

Medicinal marvel

It is probably no exaggeration to say that many of us are alive today because our ancestors discovered the healing powers of garlic. Before the introduction of antibiotics and other modern disease inhibitors, what more powerful defence did our predecessors have at their disposal? The history of garlic's use as a natural remedy is likely about as long as the history of humans itself. We can't be sure precisely how prehistoric cultures used the plant – perhaps to flavor food and as an early first-aid kit to fight common infections – but there is evidence of its importance to ancient civilizations dating back 3,000 years. Artifacts and written records from ancient Europe, China and India all confirm that garlic was widely used as a food and a healing herb: the connection between food and health was clearly understood.

"Let food be your medicine and medicine be your food,"

explained Hippocrates, the ancient Greek physician and father of modern medicine, in the fifth century.

It is only since the appearance of modern antibiotics at the beginning of the 20th century that garlic lost its place in the doctor's black bag. Until then, garlic preparations were regularly prescribed to combat many common illnesses. These days many people have a new curiosity and interest in natural remedies. Antibiotics have been overprescribed to the point of endangering their effectiveness and so there is new interest in garlic's natural antibacterial, antifungal and antiviral action, which makes it an extremely effective cure and preventative measure.

Garlic's history of health

Garlic in ancient Europe

The Egyptians held garlic in high reverence as both a medicinal and a spiritual food (see Mystery and Magic, opposite). In the *Ebers Papyrus*, a medical text dating from c.1550BC, garlic is cited as a remedy for more than 20 ailments, including headaches, throat infections, physical weakness, heart problems, tumors and animal and insect bites. The Greek historian Herodotus, who visited Egypt in 450BC, noted that the builders of the great pyramids had eaten vast quantities of garlic as they believed it brought both energy and strength.

In Greece and Rome, warriors and Olympian athletes consumed garlic to give them strength, endurance and courage, and writings show that it was widely used in medicinal preparations. Hippocrates recommended garlic for settling upset stomachs, curing infections and inflammations, and driving out excess water from the body. Discorides, an authority on plants and medicines and author of *Materia Medica*, used garlic as a remedy for asthma, jaundice, toothache, skin problems, worms and as an antidote to poisons. He also foreshadowed its use for cardiovascular problems by declaring that garlic could clear the arteries. The Roman scientist and historian Pliny the Elder documented detailed information about the cultivation, storage and uses of garlic. He writes that it had powerful properties and, although esteemed by some, was especially used by country people – most popularly to repel serpents, scorpions and other beasts, treat poisonous bites, improve circulation, stimulate sexual desire and cure suspected tumors.

386. Römische Soldaten.

Gladiatoral strength

Roman generals fed their armies garlic in the belief that it gave them courage. Garlic was also planted in the fields of the countryside they conquered in the belief that courage could be passed up through the battlefield. In fact, so strong was the association between going to battle and consuming garlic, the saying "May you not eat garlic" came to mean "May you not be called up to join the army."

Garlic in ancient China and India

Garlic was first introduced to China about 2,000 years ago during the Han Dynasty. It was, and still is, considered to be a precious and health-inducing warming herb. One of the earliest and most respected texts on traditional Chinese medicine is the *Huang Di Neijing* (*The Yellow Emperor's Classic of Internal Medicine*), written by the Yellow Emperor (Huang Di), the father of Chinese medicinal knowledge. According to the book, garlic is "warming in nature and has an affinity towards the stomach and spleen, heart, small intestine, lungs and large intestine."

Today, Chinese herbal medicine practitioners recommend garlic for numerous conditions, including abscesses and warts, asthma, hay fever, diarrhea, dysentery, enteritis, hepatitis, tuberculosis, poor circulation, the common cold, pneumonia, snake bites, unfavorable bacteria and yeasts, worms and viruses associated with degenerative diseases such as cancer.

In Ayurvedic medicine, which originated in India more than 5,000 years ago, garlic has been highly valued as a treatment for countless conditions — its ancient Sanskrit name is *mahanshadha* (panacea). The ancient Ayurvedic text *Charaka Samhita* (written c.400BC–200BC) recommends garlic for heart disease and arthritis. Other uses are similar to those found in traditional Chinese medicine and include coughs and mucus conditions, stomach and liver disorders, high blood pressure, parasites, pneumonia, rheumatism, sexual problems, tuberculosis, wounds and ulcers.

Mystery and magic

Before science was able to explain garlic's curative abilities, people put its healing powers down to pure magic. Since garlic was so effective at fighting off disease, it was used against spiritual ills too. Tales of its use as a force against evil are widespread throughout the world:

• Ancient Egyptians bestowed many sacred qualities on garlic. To ward off evil spirits, they buried garlic-shaped lumps of clay with their dead pharaohs. (Archaeologists found several bulbs of garlic, dried and almost perfectly preserved, in the tomb of Tutankhamen, buried in 1500BC.) Ancient Egyptians also chewed garlic before making a journey at night, believing their bad breath would form a protective barrier against evil. Some historians believe garlic was so spiritually important to the Egyptians that they swore oaths by it.

• In ancient Greece, travelers would place garlic at crossroads to confuse the demons and cause them to lose their way. Greek midwives prepared birthing rooms by crushing a clove of garlic, and after delivering a baby, the midwife would place a necklace with a clove of garlic around the baby's neck. In the light of garlic's proven effect against the hospital superbug MRSA (methicillin-resistant *Staphylococcus aureus*), perhaps today's midwives should take note!

• For centuries, Europeans used garlic to ward off demons, werewolves and bloodsucking vampires. European peasants in the 1700s would attach braids of garlic to the entrance of their homes to ensure that dark forces would not enter. The popularization of garlic's claim to ward off vampires was largely thanks to Bram Stoker's portrayal of Count Dracula in his 1897 Gothic horror novel.

Garlic from the Middle Ages to the 19th century

Garlic continued to be used as a food and medicine in medieval and Renaissance Europe, although as time progressed it grew less popular as a culinary condiment and physicians became more selective about its medicinal applications. The Renaissance herbalist William Turner wrote in his treatise *A New Herball* that "Garleke is not only good meat but also good medicine," while his contemporary John Gerard warned that garlic's hot and drying properties made it unsuitable for some people, depending on their general constitution. However, it was praised as a protection against bites from venomous beasts, as well as warding off plagues and pestilence that were then commonplace.

Throughout 18th-century England, garlic was included in many pharmaceutical ingredients, most commonly macerated in honey, oil, vinegar or wine and applied internally or externally – herbalists today still prescribe such preparations for colds, coughs and other chest

Saved from the plague

History is rich with tales of garlic's healing power. One of the most impressive is the tale of the four thieves. In 1720 the bubonic plague that hit Marseille in southern France was so severe that citizens dared not even go near the corpses. Four convicts condemned to death were charged with the removal of the bodies. Despite their proximity to the disease, they all survived – and became wealthy on the loot they removed from the dead. When questioned, they put their survival down to drinking copious amounts of red wine in which garlic had been soaked. Today in Marseilles you can still buy a similar garlic-infused concoction – Le Vinaigre des Quatres Voleurs (Four Thieves' Vinegar).

complaints. In his *Medical Botany* the eminent physician William Woodville describes garlic's medicinal uses and warnings for people with different physical conditions, summarizing its main medical uses as an ear infection remedy, asthmas and other pulmonary disorders treatment, a diuretic for edema, an external application to remove tumors and an expeller of worms. Cloves were consumed whole, chopped up or crushed into pills.

Garlic and modern medicine

The First World War heralded the first significant role for garlic in modern medicine, when doctors had great success using it to treat gunshot wounds and fight infection. After the discovery of penicillin in 1928, natural remedies such as garlic became somewhat neglected and yet the healing herb once again came to the rescue in the Second World War, when British and Russian armies suffered a shortage of penicillin and instead used diluted garlic preparations to disinfect open wounds.

In the mid-1940s scientists began to unlock the healing secrets of the garlic plant when they discovered that it contained allicin, a sulfur compound found to have significant antibiotic, antifungal and antiviral properties. The bulb also contains many other beneficial sulfurous compounds, as well as notable vitamins, minerals and antioxidants, although exactly how these contribute to garlic's extensive healing effects has yet to be fully understood. Numerous scientific studies have supported the usefulness of garlic as a medicine and as they continue to prove its worth, there is an increasing awareness and appreciation of this powerful ancient remedy.

Daily dose

Whether your aim is to reduce your cholesterol or simply to avoid common colds, it is a good idea to maintain a frequent intake of garlic. You can add a clove or two to your cooking, but it will lose a degree of its potency. For the most powerful medicinal effect, a daily dose of raw garlic is best. The World Health Organization (WHO) recommends 1 clove (¼ oz) of raw garlic a day to promote general health. I would suggest 1–2 cloves a day as a preventative dose.

As with all herbal remedies, you may not see the benefits of consuming garlic immediately. Unlike pharmaceutical drugs, garlic works gently with the body's natural defences and gradually treats the root of the problem, which may have been developing over a long period of time. In some cases, garlic can provide quick relief – from the symptoms of a cold or from intestinal disorders, for example. But a daily dose will bring long-term health benefits. (You can increase the dose to help fight off short-term illnesses or when your immunity is particularly low.) However, garlic is not a miracle cure; your general health will only improve with positive lifestyle choices such as a healthy diet and regular exercise.

How to take it

Since chewing raw cloves first thing in the morning probably won't appeal (and it's not a good idea to eat garlic on an empty stomach), you can make it more palatable by trying one of the following:

- Crush or bash garlic into a small amount of olive oil then spread it on bread or toast.
- For children and others who are sensitive to garlic's fiery nature, place a slice between two thin slices of apple to reduce its heat.
- Buy empty pill capsules from your local health food shop, fill them with crushed raw garlic and swallow with water.
- Include raw garlic in your everyday meals – see Chapter 1 (Cooking and recipes) for delicious recipes that include a good amount of raw garlic.

Listen to your body

While overall results of garlic's medicinal benefits are very positive, its effects may differ from person to person. Some may experience a very dramatic therapeutic effect, while others may not see much of an improvement. It is important to use your discretion and choose a treatment that you feel will best suit your body. By consuming a couple of cloves of garlic a day, most people run no risk of serious side effects and are likely to enjoy better health so it's well worth the experiment.

The World Health Organization
(WHO) recommends 1 clove
(½ oz) of raw garlic a day
to promote general health.
I would suggest 1–2 cloves
a day as a preventative dose.

Garlic safety

For the majority of us, garlic is extremely safe to consume. Millions of people eat a couple of cloves a day with no ill effects. However, occasionally it can cause allergies and certain circumstances require caution.

- Those who are allergic to plants in the lily family should avoid garlic.
- Those with sensitive stomachs should be cautious when consuming raw garlic as it can cause mild indigestion, flatulence and sometimes diarrhea. To avoid gastrointestinal problems, it is better not to eat garlic on an empty stomach. More serious side effects will only occur when vast quantities are consumed as its pungency can irritate the stomach lining. This can cause stomach injuries in the same way that hot chili peppers might. If you are concerned that you may react badly, start with a very small amount – a quarter or half a clove eaten with other food – then gradually build up your intake.
- Garlic should be avoided by people who are prone to stomach conditions, such as ulcers, as it can exacerbate the condition or cause new ones.
- Garlic slows blood clotting so should be avoided by pregnant women and people anticipating surgery or dental procedures as it could cause excessive bleeding. People who are taking anticoagulant drugs such as warfarin should consult their doctor before consuming garlic regularly, especially in raw form.
- Some studies suggest that garlic can lower blood-sugar levels and increase insulin.
- Garlic applied directly to the skin can cause chemical burns, contact dermatitis (rash) and bronchial asthma. It is important to patch test for any allergic reaction first and avoid leaving garlic in contact with the skin for too long. Be especially careful when treating children's skin.
- Fresh raw garlic in olive oil is at high risk of developing botulism if left at room temperature. It should be refrigerated immediately and used as quickly as possible. However, garlic in vinegar is completely safe as the high acidity prevents bacteria from incubating.

Garlic supplements

The market for health supplements continues to grow and worldwide garlic product sales are now worth over $15,000,000 USD. The variety of products is also increasing, as is the confusion over which ones bring the best health benefits. In the health supplements industry there remains a certain amount of controversy over which of garlic's compounds is responsible for its therapeutic properties, so the products retain different active ingredients that have varying degrees of medicinal value. The advantages of garlic supplements is that they have some or all of the odor removed and offer a measured dose. However, not all the information on the products is comprehensive and unbiased, and not all preparations list accurate measures of what they contain. My preference has always been for the most natural route – consuming the clove – but given there is a high demand for garlic supplements, here is an overview of the types available and some insight into their relative effectiveness.

Garlic oil

Garlic oil is made in a similar way to other essential oils. There are two different methods for its preparation. One involves steam-distilling mashed garlic, so capturing the oil released as the allicin breaks down. Vegetable oil is then added to the garlic oil to dilute it to a more economical and useable concentration. Alternatively, vegetable oil is added to mashed garlic without heating it. The oil is then filtered to remove the garlic solids. This is called garlic macerate oil. The two methods result in quite different benefits. On the positive side, steam-distilled garlic oil has been shown to be an effective enhancer of the immune system and to have mild antibiotic qualities. Garlic oil macerate, on the other hand, has a stronger antibiotic effect and is far more beneficial for cardiovascular health.

Taking garlic oil may reduce some of the odors associated with eating raw garlic but some odor may still emerge as the capsule dissolves in the stomach and releases odorous compounds through the lungs and skin. There

are a number of garlic oils available, all of which vary in their composition and manufacturing method. If you are interested in trying garlic oil, check the amount of actual garlic oil contained in the capsule, which usually comprises a small amount of garlic oil diluted in vegetable oil. Keep in mind that a clove of garlic will produce 2–6mg oil and many capsules available on the market contain less than 1mg.

Garlic powder

This is made by drying sliced or crushed garlic, then grinding it into a powder and forming it into capsules that can be coated to reduce garlic odor. Clinical trials of these products have produced very positive results, especially in cardiovascular health. However, not all garlic powders are the same and their potency will largely depend on how they have been prepared. Special conditions are necessary to ensure the powder retains garlic's active ingredients. Properly processed powder needs to contain both alliin and alliinase, which once hydrated will interact to produce allicin. The best way to test these products is simply to taste the powder contained within the capsule. If there is allicin present, it will be pungent and create a burning sensation on the tongue. The greater the sensation, the more allicin is present.

Some garlic capsules will state the allicin content on the packaging, but in fact it is not entirely helpful to know this. Since some of the allicin may be destroyed by stomach acids, it is the allicin "potential" that is useful. Some manufacturers have tried to resolve this by covering pills with an enteric coating, which allows the capsule to pass through the stomach without dissolving until it reaches the small intestine. Coatings vary from product to product, as will the acidity of each person's stomach. There is always a risk that it may not dissolve at all and will therefore be excreted without allowing any allicin into the body.

Aged garlic extract

Particularly popular in Japan, aged garlic extract (AGE) relies on a completely different principle to other supplements. It is made from whole or sliced garlic that is aged in alcohol for a number of months. The objective is to remove allicin and almost all its derivations, making the preparation completely odorless. The manufacturers of AGE claim that allicin is "dangerous," and it is the few specific sulfur compounds created when garlic is aged in alcohol that produce therapeutic benefits. However, there is a strong debate about the effectiveness of these deodorized garlic products. The majority of clinical and scientific research shows AGE to be more beneficial in the area of cancer prevention, while other garlic preparations are better at maintaining cardiovascular health.

Keep it natural

With no standardized labeling, regulation or testing of these products, it is difficult to determine their reliability to live up to specific health claims. In theory, a combination of supplements could produce a number of useful therapeutic effects. On the other hand, we can be certain that fresh garlic offers the best and most potent allicin content, so if you enjoy its pungent aroma and flavor, the simplest and cheapest way of accessing its healing potential is to add it to your food.

No stink, no benefit

Crude as it may seem, there appears to be an element of truth in the claim that a discernible odor after consuming garlic indicates that it is being effectively used by our bodies. The important thing to notice is the secondary odor that is released a few hours after consuming garlic. This can be relatively mild compared with garlic breath from eating raw and cooked cloves but it shows that the oil-soluble compounds (sulfides) have been absorbed and are circulating in the body's system.

Antidotes to garlic odors

What a shame that some people are reluctant to eat large amounts of garlic for fear of garlic breath, and those who do indulge in a delicious garlic-saturated meal will then desperately brush their teeth or suck on mints, paranoid that they might breathe garlic on their neighbors. Of course, if you're constantly surrounded by garlic you don't tend to notice the odd whiff, but understandably it's not too desirable for those returning to a crowded office or who may be out on a first date.

So what causes the dreaded smell and how can you avoid it? When we eat garlic, our bodies produce a number of sulfur-containing gases that are produced by natural changes in allicin, the active sulfur compound in garlic. Most of these gases are metabolized by the body except for allyl methyl sulfide (AMS). The liver and intestines cannot metabolize AMS so it ends up finding its way out of the body in our breath and other secretions. When we eat fresh garlic, the odor comes initially from the mouth, then from the stomach and finally through the lungs and skin. However, there are a few things you can do to avoid offending other people:

- Eat more garlic! This may seem counterintuitive, but there is evidence to suggest that the more we eat, the easier it is for our bodies to metabolize it.
- Chew a roasted coffee bean.
- Eat a couple of slices of lemon to help neutralize the odors.
- Brush your teeth and tongue with toothpaste or baking soda.
- Chew parsley leaves. The only downside to this is you can then spend hours picking it out of your teeth!
- Drink a cereal grass drink such as wheatgrass juice (available in health food shops) after eating garlic. As well as neutralizing its odor, it helps reduce the burning sensation in the lining of the digestive tract.
- If you are consuming crushed raw garlic as a daily dose for health purposes, you can reduce the odor by swallowing it without chewing. Make a pill by putting the crushed garlic into an empty pill capsule, available from health food stores.
- Spread the word! Make sure all those around you also eat garlic. Not only is it good for them, they are less likely to notice the garlic scent.

Garlic and modern medicine: conditions and cures

Written records of the last few centuries contain numerous references to garlic's use as a natural medicine, but which of these still hold value to us today? Let's have a look at the evidence for garlic's main medicinal claims, from historical traditions to current scientific research.

"Garlic is a veritable pharmacopeia. That's why garlic has been found in every medical book of every culture ever."

Dr Herbert Pierson, former director of the National Cancer Institute's "Designer Foods" program

Bites and stings

Many references in traditional medicine suggest garlic's use as a first-aid remedy against assaults from bug bites and stings. Modern science has taught us that although garlic can be of some limited use in stopping the spread of stings or venom, this is not its trump card. Thankfully, we now have access to correct anti-venoms for serious bites and stings so I strongly recommend seeking them out rather than using garlic! We also know that pain or irritation from minor bites from mosquitoes, for example, is due to inflammation, so garlic has limited use once bites and stings have occurred. As an antidote, garlic may be used as a last-resort remedy to help slow the spread of stings from bees or wasps or venom from snakes or scorpions, but in the latter cases the correct anti-venom should be sought.

Garlic works better as a deterrent rather than as an antidote for most bites and stings. Regular consumption of garlic is an effective repellent to mosquitoes and gnats: a small amount of sulfur released in the perspiration after eating garlic prevents insects from biting. Alternatively, a solution of garlic and water or garlic crushed into petroleum jelly and applied to the skin is helpful in warding off all types of insects. Indian women add garlic to the oil they rub on their hair to keep head lice away. Rubbing garlic into your children's hair before school may create worse problems than lice, but for pets it can be an ideal way to keep their coat free from fleas, ticks and lice. Combining garlic with your pet's food is another way to repel such parasites.

Cardiovascular disease and poor circulation

Diorcorides, the ancient Greek physician and author of *De Materia Medica* (*Regarding Medical Materials*), claimed that garlic cleared the arteries and the ancient Egyptian *Ebers Papyrus* also suggested the use of garlic to improve circulation. The influential Ayurvedic medical text *Charaka Samhita*, written more than 2,000 years ago, recommended garlic for the treatment of heart disease, and in Asian medicine garlic was specifically used to remove fat from the blood and dry out excess moisture from the body. In England in the late 16th century, garlic was recommended as a cure for dropsy, where part of the body swelled up and become waterlogged, a condition now known as edema.

Today, diseases of the heart and circulation are among the most serious health conditions. There is no quick-fix solution to these problems as they generally occur as part of a degenerative process affected by man y factors, including saturated fat in our diet, lack of exercise, smoking and stress. But there is a great deal we can do to improve our cardiovascular health with simple lifestyle changes and our good friend garlic. Extensive research has investigated the effect of garlic on all aspects of cardiovascular health, including how it can thin the blood, improve circulation, reduce cholesterol levels and lower blood pressure.

The heart of the matter

To understand how garlic can work to aid heart health, it helps to have a basic understanding of how cardiovascular problems occur. Cholesterol has been commonly named as the root cause. High levels of "bad cholesterol" or LDL (low-density lipoprotein) are closely associated with the risk of a heart attack. LDL taken up by the arteries creates fatty lumps, causing furring of the arteries that can eventually block or seriously interrupt the transit of blood. Restriction of the blood supply damages the heart muscle very quickly and can lead to a heart attack. Restricted blood supply to

There is a great deal we can do to improve our cardiovascular health with simple lifestyle changes and our good friend garlic.

the brain due to congested arteries or from a clot is known as a stroke.

HDL (high-density lipoprotein), on the other hand, is the "good cholesterol" as it actually protects from heart disease. HDL is manufactured by the liver and removes unwanted cholesterol from the walls of the arteries, returning it to the liver for disposal. Our bodies do need a small amount of cholesterol to maintain our cell membranes and make natural hormones, but keeping the correct balance of HDLs and LDLs is essential. If the LDL level is too high and HDL too low then cholesterol material will be deposited on the walls of the arteries, leading to atherosclerosis (hardening of the arteries).

We have been told that diets high in fat increase cholesterol levels and the risk of heart disease, yet statistics from across Europe reveal that this is only part of the story. In southern France, Spain and Italy, consumption of saturated fats is relatively high, but the incidence of heart disease is relatively low. Explanations for this conundrum, dubbed the "French paradox," have been sought by looking at other factors in the Mediterranean lifestyle that could have an effect on cardiovascular health. An often-quoted Canadian study conducted by Ancel Keys in 1980 investigated the effects of diets rich in wine and garlic on coronary heart disease and concluded that the more garlic a nation consumed, the lower its level of heart disease. In addition, garlic consumption was found to have a greater association with better cardiovascular health than wine drinking.

Healthy blood flow

Garlic has a two-pronged effect on circulation and heart health. It lowers blood pressure by dilating the muscles of the blood vessels, which increases blood flow and improves circulation. Consumed over the long term, it can significantly reduce cholesterol levels and is especially effective at lowering the level of harmful blood cholesterol. Garlic's effect is more pronounced when cholesterol levels are high. According to 30 clinical studies, a dose of 1–2 cloves per day (or equivalent in supplement form) was able to lower cholesterol by an average of 15 percent. This would reduce the risk of heart attack by 30 percent. These studies also concluded that garlic is most effective if regularly consumed for at least three months, a further indication that garlic should be part of our daily diet.

As well as lowering cholesterol levels, a number of studies reveal that garlic reduces blood clotting and so improves circulation, reducing the risk of thrombosis. The effect is almost immediate. Garlic works in a similar manner to aspirin, the remedy often suggested as a long-term preventative against excessive clotting. Comparative tests show that garlic is at least as effective as aspirin in achieving improved circulation.

Warning: If you are taking prescribed anti-coagulant drugs such as warfarin, you should consult your doctor before taking any garlic supplements or eating large quantities of raw garlic.

Improved virility

For centuries many cultures have hailed garlic as an aphrodisiac due to its ability to boost blood circulation. Some men with heart disease may suffer from impotence due to poor circulation and narrowing of the arteries in the groin. By aiding blood flow, garlic can act like a natural Viagra and is commonly prescribed by Ayurvedic practitioners to increase virility.

Cancer

With current statistics suggesting one in three people will develop cancer at some time in their life, one of the most exciting prospects for garlic's therapeutic use is as a potential anticancer agent. While modern medicine is constantly finding new and better ways to combat the disease, we are coming to realize that natural alternatives have much to offer too. Preliminary studies suggest that garlic consumption may reduce the risk of developing several types of cancer, especially those associated with the gastrointestinal tract. Both the National Cancer Institute (NCI) in the US and the World Health Organization (WHO) recognize garlic as having potential anticancer properties.

It seems that garlic is one of the most ancient spice plants reputed to have an effect on cancer. Ancient Egyptian physicians applied garlic externally for the treatment of tumors, as recorded in the *Ebers Papyrus* c.1550BC, while the Greek physician Hippocrates and ancient Indian physicians applied it internally. The earliest modern scientific confirmation of garlic's value as an anticancer agent was an experiment conducted in 1958, when US researchers Weisberger and Pensky successfully demonstrated that garlic extracts inhibited the growth of tumor cells.

Most recently, population studies have been used to test the effectiveness of garlic in cancer prevention and the evidence is promising. A number of these studies show an association between an increased intake of garlic and reduced risk of certain cancers, including cancers of the stomach, colon, esophagus, pancreas and breast. Clinical trials conducted so far are few and further studies are needed, but the results are encouraging.

So how does garlic act to prevent cancer? Studies so far point to a number of factors. As with other infectious diseases, garlic's role in stimulating the immune system may be part of the explanation. The vitamins and minerals in garlic, like selenium and vitamin C, which enhance the action of the body's natural killer cells are also antioxidants,

which protect from harmful free radicals and attack tumor cells before cancers can develop. A review of current research by the National Cancer Institute suggests other possible reasons, including its antibacterial properties, its ability to block the formation of cancer-causing substances, enhance DNA repair, slow down cell reproduction and induce cell death.

Garlic by no means offers a simple anticancer cure, but when consumed regularly and in reasonable quantities, it clearly has a profound impact on our bodies' ability to keep certain cancers at bay.

Heavy metal toxicity

In our modern world, heavy metal pollution is a global problem that is a growing threat to humanity. Heavy metal toxicity is the silent destroyer: seldom reported but largely damaging to our health. Exposure to heavy metals is usually connected with areas of intense industry, yet road travel is also a widespread source of heavy metals, with lead, zinc, iron, copper, cadmium, chromium, nickel and aluminium commonly found in road run-off. Lead poisoning is now falling in industrialized countries, where lead is no longer used in plumbing systems, petrol and food packaging. But we are still exposed to other heavy metals such as mercury through pesticides, wood preservatives, some medicines and contaminated fish. Heavy metals are a concern because at high levels our bodies are not able to metabolize them. They accumulate in the soft tissues and cause nutritional problems and other debilitating chronic conditions. For example, mercury poisoning can cause, among other symptoms, anxiety, mood swings and antisocial behavior. The phrase "mad as a hatter" is derived from poisoning among hat makers who used mercuric nitrate to soften the hair of animal hides.

Research scientists at the Indian Institute of Chemical Biology found that garlic can act as an antidote to heavy metal poisoning, showing effectiveness in reducing levels of cadmium, arsenic, copper, mercury and lead. Garlic has a dual defense against heavy metals in the body. Since it is rich in sulfur compounds, which have purifying properties, it can act as a "sulfur donor," providing organic sulfur to the body to help detoxification. Garlic's antioxidant activity can also reduce oxidative stress caused by heavy metal toxicity which can damage or destroy the cell walls within the body and potentially lead to cancer. In some cases, the curative effect of garlic was found to be superior to pharmaceutical remedies. The precise way in which garlic works to achieve protection against heavy metals is still not wholly understood, but given that current synthetic drugs can have harmful side effects, garlic presents an attractive natural alternative.

Infections

Traditionally, garlic was used to treat both internal and external infections. It was commonly prescribed for internal conditions of the ears, mouth, skin, stomach and throat, and applied externally to treat boils, spots and ulcers. During the First and Second World Wars garlic was used to treat open wounds, and troops in the trenches relied on garlic as protection against gangrene and as a cure for dysentery. In China and India, garlic has long been recommended for cholera, dysentery and as an antiseptic lotion for washing wounds and ulcers.

Garlic's anti-infective power is now supported by a huge amount of scientific evidence. The first to demonstrate it was the French chemist and microbiologist Louis Pasteur, in 1858. When he grew bacteria in a culture dish, he found garlic juice managed to kill all the bacteria around it. Throughout the last century, numerous similar laboratory tests were conducted to test garlic's effectiveness against disease-causing bacteria and yeasts. The results overwhelmingly show that garlic can work against a variety of bacteria and fungi, including Candida (see page 106), Cryptococcus (which causes meningitis), Microsporum (ringworm) and Salmonella.

Apart from having fewer side effects, garlic's overwhelming advantage over antibiotics is two-fold. First, it does not create bacterial resistance in the way

Immunity booster

In the face of viral diseases with no known effective cures or treatments, we rely heavily on our body's immunity to fight off infection. Poor diets, environmental pollution, stress and the general pressure of modern life all have a negative effect on the working of our immune system, leaving us more vulnerable to disease and less able to fight off infections in the body.

Several studies have tested garlic's immune-stimulating properties and have conclusively proved garlic's role in boosting the body's defences. As eloquently described by *The Journal of the American Medical Association*, "Garlic may become known as one of the grand conductors of the body's immune symphony." However, scientists have yet to understand exactly which component is responsible. Garlic's ability to pick up toxic materials and transport them out of the body due to the detoxifying/dispersing effects of its sulfur compounds (see Heavy metal toxicity, left) may partly explain. In effect by consuming garlic we are using the plant's natural defence mechanism against our own viruses. Allicin combined with other nutrients present in garlic — such as vitamins B1, B3, B6 and C, and minerals germanium, phosphorous and selenium — all contribute to making garlic one of the best immune-system fortifiers available.

Immune-boosting soup

This clear broth does wonders if you're feeling congested and makes a very effective immune booster too. The large amount of garlic may surprise you, but trust me the flavor is fantastic. Shiitake mushrooms are a symbol of longevity in Asia and an excellent source of selenium, a known antioxidant that plays a vital role in boosting the immune system.

30 g (1 oz) dried shiitake, porcini and oyster mushrooms
    (add extra fresh shiitake mushrooms if available)
15 ml (1 tablespoon) olive oil
1 medium white onion, finely chopped
a thumb-sized piece of ginger, peeled and grated
1 whole garlic bulb, peeled
15 ml (1 tablespoon) vegetable bouillon powder
    or 1 vegetable stock cube
juice of 1 lemon
sea salt
freshly ground black pepper to taste

Serves 4

1. Pour boiling water (about 250 ml/1 cup) over the dried mushrooms in a bowl and leave them to soak for 10 minutes.
2. In the meantime, heat the oil in a heavy-based ovenproof pan. Add the onion and ginger then crush in all the garlic cloves. Fry gently until softened and aromatic.
3. Add the mushrooms and their water to the pan, plus any fresh mushrooms, then stir in the stock and the lemon juice.
4. Season, then gently simmer with the lid on for at least 2 hours. Alternatively, transfer the pan the oven on low heat (about 250°F). Season to taste before serving with crusty bread.

antibiotics do; there is no evidence that bacteria become so accustomed to garlic that they start to live with it or even on it. Second, garlic has the ability to act on a range of bacterial and fungal infections rather than targeting specific bugs. It does not work as precisely or as quickly as antibiotics, but has a gentle and persistent action on the body. For this reason it is ideally suited to the treatment of infections that are not acute or immediately life threatening. Bacterial problems of the chest, gums, skin, throat and stomach all respond well to garlic. Fungal and yeast infections, such as athlete's foot, Candida (see below), cystitis, vaginitis, thrush and ringworm, are also suitable for treatment. The latter can be quite relentless and hard to tackle with modern drugs, which often meddle with the body's own immunity. As well as eliminating unfavorable yeasts, regular consumption of garlic helps promote the growth of healthy intestinal flora.

Candida

Yeast infections plague millions of people and can cause conditions such as thrush, vaginal yeast infections and intestinal yeast disorders. Candida is an opportunistic pathogen: it thrives in human hosts with compromised immune systems. It is thought that the growing number of people suffering from Candida albicans is due in part to the overuse of antibiotics as they destroy both good and bad bacteria, giving the disease a chance to multiply, so it has become an increasing concern to find effective natural solutions. Several studies have shown the great potency of garlic against yeasts, including Candida. A 2009 study by Lemar et al., for example, showed the reduction of Candida albicans growth by introducing fresh garlic and garlic extracts.

Ear infections

Some children are particularly prone to ear infections and they can be very distressing for both the child and parents. Although antibiotics may well be necessary in severe cases, this garlic oil remedy will generally resolve simple earache (first stages of inflammation) within 24 hours. If the earache persists you should seek professional help – do not delay treatment, especially where children are concerned.

Garlic oil

Heat 1 tablespoon of olive oil in a small pan until slightly warmer than body temperature but not very hot. Remove from the heat and crush 1 large garlic clove into the hot oil. Allow the oil and garlic to cool to body temperature – a few minutes should suffice. Strain out the garlic then put a few drops of the warm oil onto a cottonball and gently place it in the opening of the ear and leave for 30–40 minutes.

If treating adults, you can try this alternative:

Chop 1 large garlic clove so the flesh is exposed then wrap it in cotton gauze to avoid direct contact with the skin, and place it over the opening of the ear canal for as long as possible. The longer you leave it, the more effective it will be. Under no circumstances must you put anything inside the ear canal – this can be dangerous for both adults and children. These preparations should be applied only to the outer ear and entrance to the ear canal.

Stomach upset

Garlic has been successful in combating even the most aggressive bacteria responsible for stomach upsets. If you have severe vomiting or diarrhea, you should seek medical advice immediately. But for mild stomach upsets, this garlic drink should get your digestive system back in healthy working order.

Warm garlic milk drink

Crush 3 large garlic cloves into 2 teaspoons of olive oil and mix into a paste. Slowly incorporate 3 tablespoons of warm milk. Add sugar or honey to taste. Stir well and drink.

Skin problems

Garlic has wonderful antiseptic properties that can be used to treat many skin conditions and external infections. There are a number of options for antiseptic applications, depending on the nature of the skin complaint:

Acne, spots or mouth ulcers
🧄 Simply hold a chopped clove against the affected area for a few minutes.

Small areas of skin such as a minor wound, boil, blemish or infection
🧄 First apply petroleum jelly to the surrounding area of skin. Crush a small amount of garlic onto a cottonball or a plaster then stick it in place and leave for 15–20 minutes while it draws out the infection and reduces any swelling. Carefully peel off and rinse with warm water. You can repeat this morning and night for as long as necessary to promote healing.

Larger areas of skin
🧄 Make a solution of 100 ml (¼ cup) warm water and 3 cloves of crushed garlic then dab onto the affected area with cotton wool. Use the solution within 3 hours as it will lose its potency over time. Always make a new solution for each application.

Planter warts
🧄 First protect the healthy skin around the wart by smearing it with petroleum jelly before applying the garlic. Thinly slice a clove of garlic then put a slice onto the wart, securing it in place with a plaster or piece of gauze and medical tape. Replace with a fresh slice of garlic daily. This method should dissolve the wart within a week.

Athlete's foot
This fungal skin infection is incredibly common and can be itchy, but applying garlic paste helps to clear it.

🧄 **Garlic paste**
Crush a few cloves of garlic into olive oil to make a paste. Leave for 24 hours before applying the oil between the toes 3–4 times a day. You can also soak a cotton ball in the paste and place it between the toes overnight. Put socks on to protect your bedding from garlic aromas! Alternatively, sprinkle powdered garlic daily on wet feet and allow to dry (socks may be worn).

Rashes
🧄 Garlic tea, applied cool with a cotton ball or by drinking, will relieve itching, painful rashes caused by poison ivy and poison oak – see the recipe on page 109 (Colds and coughs). It is also good for nettle stings.

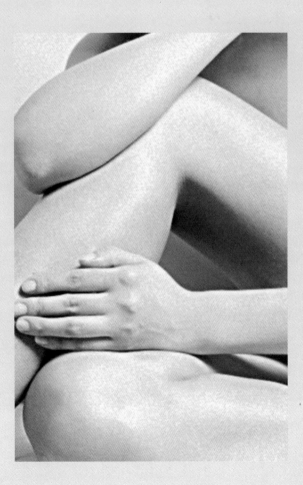

Viruses

Garlic has long been thought to possess antiviral properties and for many it reliably wards off the most prevalent viral infection of all: the common cold. Where other viruses are concerned, however, little work has been done to investigate garlic's potential. The latest research indicates that garlic extract shows positive activity against a number of viral illnesses. Among these are human rotavirus (the most common cause of stomach flu among small children), various types of herpes, viral pneumonia and even Human Immunodeficiency Virus (HIV). However, more research is needed before any firm conclusions can be reached. What is known is that garlic also has a very encouraging effect on the immune system, enabling the body to better cope with infections of all sorts.

Cold sores

While there is no known cure for the herpes virus that causes cold sores, consumption of garlic may reduce the severity and frequency of outbreaks and topical application can help to speed the healing process.

♠ Cut a clove and hold the exposed edge directly against the sore for 5–10 minutes. It's going to sting like crazy, so be prepared to grit your teeth and do not leave the garlic on the skin for longer than 10 minutes.

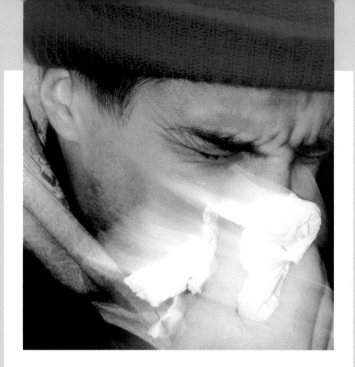

Cold cure?

I used to have an eccentric piano teacher who claimed not to have had a cold for 20 years. His secret was to eat a clove of raw garlic every day. Peter Josling, founder and director of The Garlic Centre in East Sussex, conducted a study involving 146 volunteers to test the power of garlic's active compound allicin on our defences against colds. Half took one capsule of Allicinmax, an allicin-containing garlic supplement, while the remaining volunteers took a placebo. Over a 90-day period during the winter, just 24 colds were recorded among those taking the supplement, compared with 65 among those taking the placebo. The study also found that those who did catch a cold while taking the supplement were more likely to make a speedier recovery than those taking the placebo, and the chances of reinfection following a cold were significantly reduced. Perhaps chewing a clove a day should no longer be the reserve of eccentrics but common practice. Since the average person will spend two to three years of their life with a cold, there's much to gain by a daily dose to treat colds and boost immunity.

Colds and coughs

For centuries garlic has been used as a natural antiviral to ward off symptoms of colds and respiratory infections. These basic garlic preparations will bring overall relief and resistance:

I've found that this garlic infusion will help knock a cold on the head if you drink it at the early onset of the symptoms. Or just drink it whenever you feel the need to boost your immune system.

Garlic Tea

Pour 250 ml (1 cup) boiling water over 4 large roughly chopped garlic cloves and allow them to infuse for a few minutes. Stir in the juice of ½ lemon, 1 tablespoon apple cider vinegar and honey to taste, then pour into a mug and sip the hot mixture. For maximum benefits, I'd recommend scooping out the chopped cloves from the bottom of the mug and eating those too. Don't worry — they'll be much milder than raw garlic.

Garlic-infused water can also make an excellent inhalant.

● Garlic inhalant

Put 4 cloves of chopped garlic into a large bowl, pour over a kettleful of boiling water then add a tablespoon of apple cider vinegar. Place a towel over your head and the bowl, and inhale the vapors for at least 5 minutes.

Chesty coughs

My rather evangelistic approach to garlic has had our household trying all sorts of garlic concoctions to test their effects. Although my husband is a happy guinea pig, he did raise an eyebrow when I started rubbing garlic oil into our toddler's feet before bed. While he remains a little sceptical, I'm convinced that the horrible cough had subsided by the morning.

The skin is the largest organ in the body and is often disregarded as a way of absorbing nutrients. The feet do a great job of absorbing the active ingredients of garlic into the bloodstream. In fact, this method is so effective, you can smell garlic on the breath shortly after applying the rub.

◖ Garlic oil foot rub

Garlic can be quite astringent if applied directly to the skin, so it is best to mix it with oil, such as jojoba or sweet almond, before applying it to any part of the body.

Sore throats and wheezy coughs

This soothing syrup is similar to garlic tea but stronger and thicker in texture to help reach the spot.

◖ Garlic syrup

In a small bowl, crush 8 large garlic cloves and mash into a paste before adding 8 teaspoons apple cider vinegar. Refrigerate overnight or for at least 4 hours. The next day, warm 3 tablespoons of honey and add it to the garlic vinegar mixture before stirring in 4 teaspoons of lemon juice. Store in the fridge until required.

For a sore throat, take 2 teaspoons of the mixture. Retain it in the mouth, allowing the syrup to reach the tonsils, before gargling and swallowing. Repeat 2–3 times a day. For a cough, take 2–3 teaspoons morning and night. Make your excuses to your bedfellow as I'm afraid this one does have odorous side effects.

What is garlic?

The beauty of garlic

Have you ever marveled at the natural beauty of a garlic plant? Bulbs with bright white, mauve-tinged or purple skin covering firm, rounded cloves tightly clasped together at a curly mess of roots; a long elegant stem topped with spear-shaped leaves. No wonder it attracts attention like no other plant.

Intriguingly, a sniff of its exterior reveals only a hint of the spectacular strong aroma, flavors and potent healing power hidden within. But break open a clove and you open a portal to unimagined sensory delights and health benefits. The underlying beauty of garlic resides in its unique chemical composition, which holds secrets it has us taken centuries to unfold.

The culinary and medicinal value of garlic has been prized in almost all cultures for thousands of years and yet our understanding of how garlic works owes much to the last century of scientific study. Our growing interest in complementary and alternative medicine has led to a burst of garlic research in recent years and the results have been fascinating. Over 2200 credible scientific papers have been published on all aspects of garlic, including its chemistry, pharmacology and clinical applications, and they unanimously point to the humble clove as an amazing resource of phytochemicals (botanicals) with a wide range of curative and preventative powers that are of incredible value in today's world.

Garlic's origins and diaspora

Garlic has been well established in many cultures for thousands of years. The earliest record of garlic's use in human culture was discovered in El Mahasna in Egypt when archaeologists excavated a tomb dating back to 3750BC. Here they found a collection of garlic bulbs modeled in clay, a clue to both the real and symbolic value of this plant in Egyptian culture. This is as far back as we can trace it definitively, but with this proof that garlic had attained such extraordinary status by this point in history, we can deduce that it was highly prized and widely traded for some time before. Yet where did it come from?

The hunt for the origins of garlic became swept up in the 19th-century enthusiasm for botanical exploration. Eduard August von Regel, a prominent German horticulturalist and botanist, devoted his career to identifying plants from the Russian Far East and Asia and reported seeing specimens of wild garlic from the Dzungaria Basin, a Central Asian area north of the Tien Shan mountain range in northwest China. A French–Swiss botanist, Alphonse De Candolle, took this research further and stated that the only place where garlic was shown to grow in its wild state was in "the desert of the Kirghis of Sungari" in Manchuria, southwestern Siberia. Soviet researchers continued this line of study during the cold war and were able to confirm central Asia as garlic's indigenous habitat.

The first people to discover the plant growing wild in this region were most likely nomadic hunter-gatherers who came across species of the onion family (the *genus Allium*) growing as the snows melted in the spring. The bulbs had varying degrees of onion flavor, but one in particular would have stood out because of its intense, fiery taste – the plant now botanically classified as *Allium longicuspis* – wild garlic. Bulbs were likely gathered in the summer, conserved, and then used to flavor food as well as to make medicinal preparations, and in this way, garlic soon became an indispensable part of the hunter-gatherers' diet. Bulbs, being lightweight and long-lasting, were ideally suited to the nomadic lifestyle, accompanying them on their travels and in turn, helping the bulb make its journey around the world.

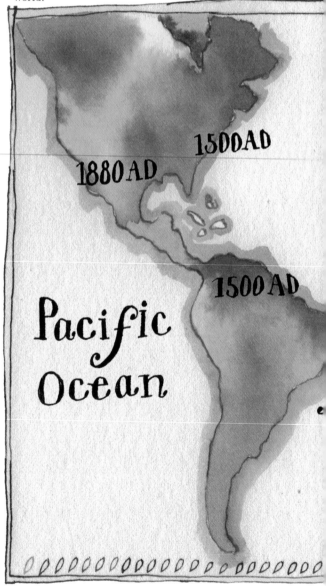

The map below illustrates how far garlic travelled beyond its point of origin in Central Asia. The timeline lists the key dates that enable us to plot this journey.

Key:

10,000BC: The Garlic Crescent End of the last Ice Age. *Allium longicuspis*, progenitor of the garlic we know today grows in small pockets along the Tien Shan mountains. Small hunter-gatherer groups carry it out of the area.

5,000BC: Garlic reaches Mesopotamia and is recorded on cuneiforms (clay tablets) in the first cities in the valleys of the Euphrates and Tigris rivers

3,000BC: First records of garlic's use in Ancient Egypt

1,000BC: First records of garlic's use in China

500BC: Garlic mentioned in Ancient Greek literature and medicinals

100BC: Garlic mentioned in Etruscan and early Latin texts in Italy

42AD: Arrival of garlic in Britain with the Roman Conquest

500AD: Established within the old Roman Empire

1500AD: Carried by the Spanish to North and South America

1880: First Garlic production in Gilroy California

1975: The Garlic Farm on the Isle of Wight starts growing garlic

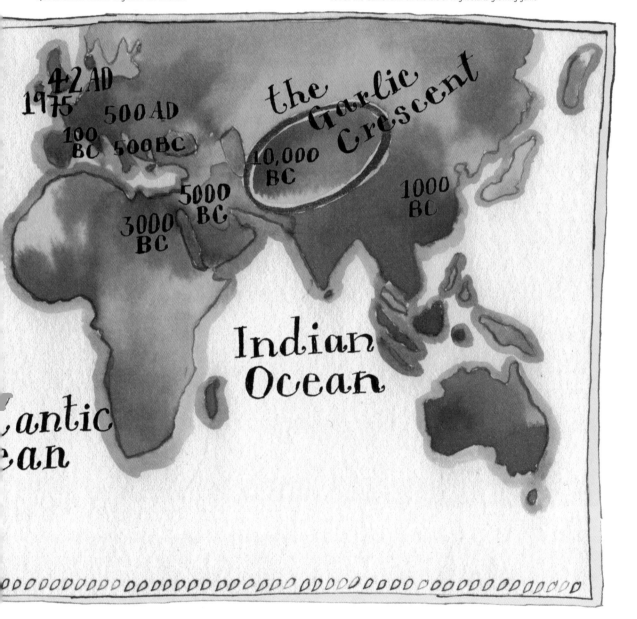

Cultivation

It is highly probable that garlic's cultivation came about as the result of an accident. We know that agriculture began around the Neolithic period, when humans began cultivating plants for food. This development brought with it a change in the hunter-gatherer lifestyle; becoming nomadic for part of the year, but returning to a region to reap their harvest. Upon arrival in a new area in autumn, garlic bulbs were no doubt stored in the ground for later retrieval. However, on the hunter-gatherers' return the following summer, the bulbs would have multiplied, thus revealing the secret to garlic's cultivation. Trade among agricultural communities helped spread food crops far beyond their point of origin and garlic was destined to travel far, growing as it did along one of the major trade routes of the ancient world.

Caption: (top) A Chinese farmer carrying a string of garlic
(left) A man selling garlic at a market in Yuncheng, Shanxi Province of China
(bottom) Nepalese workers unload sacks of garlic from a van at a vegetable market in the Kalimati District of Kathmandu

Garlic explorer

For my father, garlic is more than the family business, it's his passion, and in recent years he has taken it to new extremes, travelling the globe for his love of the little white bulb. Inspired by a meeting with the late Professor William Stearn, Lindley professor at Kew and a world-famous botanist and taxonomist, he began his quest for "the Mother of all Garlic." The professor gave my father two leads. First, he recommended he read the works of Bertholdt Laufer (1874–1934), one-time curator of the Chicago Field Museum and an intrepid explorer of Central Asia; second, he suggested he travel to Gatersleben and look up Peter Hanelt, the world authority on alliums with a lifetime's experience of travelling around the old Soviet bloc. His passion fired up even further by this quest, my father eventually followed in Peter Hanelt's footsteps, travelling to Kazakhstan, the Caucasus and Eastern Turkey and, with the assistance of the great Russian botanist, Anna Ivashenko, eventually found his holy grail *Allium longicuspis* and *Allium tuncelianum*, generally held to be the wild progenitors of *Allium sativum*, the garlic we grow today.

Caption: (top) Indian laborers Raju (L) and Ali fill bags with garlic at a vegetable market before exporting them to Pakistan through the border town of Wagah. (bottom) An aromatic herbs and garlic seller near the Maubert street market in 1956

Selection

Allium longicuspis is classified as a "hardneck" garlic, in that it has a woody flower stalk that produces a flower head with viable seeds, allowing it to reproduce naturally in the wild. However, as cultivation of *allium longicuspis* became widespread, growers noticed that occasional growth deviations, when the plant grew with no flower stalk, had the effect of directing all the plant's energy down into the bulb, thus resulting in bigger growth. In turn, growers selected these larger bulbs to propagate the following year as they gave a far better return on the effort involved. And so it seems possible that, through this process of selection of bulbs with no flowering head, over many years the first cultivated softneck garlic came into being – *Allium sativum*.

Allium sativum has been cultivated by humans for so long that it has lost the ability to produce viable seed. Instead of fertilizing itself through pollination – it reproduces by asexual propagation – bulbs are selected from the healthiest stock and their cloves planted as "seed" the following season. Within the softneck and hardneck subspecies, there are many different varieties which suit varying climatic and soil conditions depending on their origins (see Chapter 4, Growing and varieties). It is thanks to this adaptability and propensity to create new variants that garlic grows so easily in many different climates and conditions around the world.

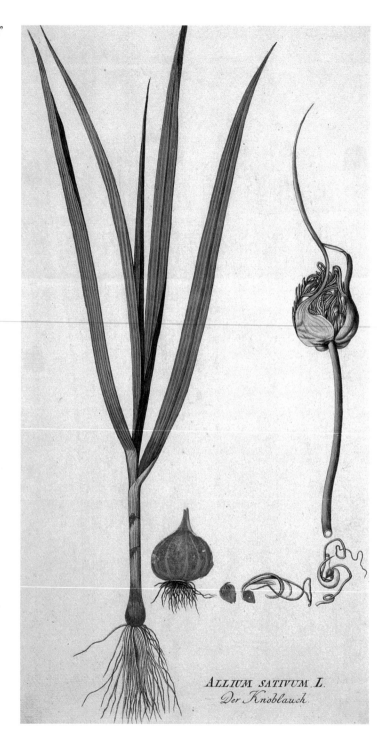

ALLIUM SATIVUM. L.
Der Knoblauch

Classification: garlic and friends

The taxonomy of garlic is as complex as it is fascinating and could fill an entire book in itself, but here is a simplified explanation of where garlic fits into the world of plants.

The word garlic is believed to originate from the Anglo Saxon *gárléac* – *gár* meaning "spear," after its pointed leaves, and *léac* meaning "leek." Known botanically as *Allium sativum* (garlic cultivated), garlic is a species of the *Allium* genus, which comprises the onion and its relatives. These belong to the lily family (*Liliaceae*), many of which are ornamental plants with attractive flowers, such as amaryllis, crocus, daffodil and hyacinth.

There are about 600 allium species, but only a few are cultivated for food, including onion, chives, shallot, rakkyo (aka Chinese onion), garlic, elephant garlic, leek and kurrat (aka Egyptian leek). All edible alliums share the common structural elements of a bulb plant and that distinctive alliaceous smell and taste we know and love.

At the heart of garlic is a true stem with a basal plate, from which tassel-like roots extend downwards. These draw moisture and nutrients from the soil and up to the true stem, where they are used to build parts of the plant. The leaves, cloves and false flower stalk (or scape) reach upwards (growing 0.3–0.6 meters/approximately 1 foot tall), seeking light and air – energy to power the growing process. Little cloves grow ever larger from the center of the plant and, as if arranged with portion control in mind, are individually wrapped in their own protective papery skin. When peeled, they reveal smooth, firm, creamy-white flesh. This is garlic's storage area and the active part of the plant. The layers of flesh form a protective coat around a young green shoot – the source of next year's growth – which can be seen if you dissect a clove that has been harvested many months before. If planted and left to develop, between four and twenty cloves will grow around this shoot, forming a new bulb.

Wild garlic

The vast majority of alliums grow in the wild and *Allium ursinum* (one of the most common) can be found carpeting damp, deciduous woodland or river valleys in the British Isles and Northern Europe. Otherwise known as ramsoms, buckrams or bear leek, the first leaves usually appear in very early spring, with star-shaped white flowers blooming toward the end of the season. Both the leaves and flowers are edible and make a delicious, fresh, mildly garlic-flavored addition to salads or can be used as a garnish or topping to risottos, pasta, chicken and fish (see chapter 1, Cooking and recipes, page 14). The leaves look very similar to those of lily of the valley, which is poisonous, but wild garlic can be easily identified by its smell – just rub the leaves between your fingers.

Another wild garlic is *Allium vineale*, or crow garlic, native to Europe, north Africa and western Asia but introduced in North America and Australia, where it has become so pervasive it is considered to be a harmful weed. Although it has a garlicky aroma, its nasty aftertaste means it has no culinary value.

What's in a clove?

A single clove of garlic is a powerhouse of more than 200 known chemical compounds, including many health-bestowing antioxidants, vitamins, minerals and sulphurous compounds. It is an excellent source of potassium, iron, calcium, magnesium, manganese, zinc, selenium and germanium, as well as antioxidants, such as beta-carotene, and vitamins B6 and C. However, its most medicinally powerful ingredient is a sulphur substance called allicin, a pungent oily liquid that the plant spontaneously creates as a defence mechanism when damaged or disturbed in some way.

Allicin is the secret to garlic's extraordinary power and explains why it has been used so effectively through the ages to preserve food and prevent and cure disease. It has been the subject of numerous scientific studies, which demonstrate its significant antibiotic, antifungal and antiviral properties. When extracted from crushed raw garlic, allicin kills bacteria or fungi on contact, and when garlic is boiled or treated so that the allicin is no longer present or active, bacteria will grow.

The complex chemistry responsible for making allicin has only begun to be explained in the last few decades. Scientists started to study garlic around the time of the industrial revolution, along with research into the chemical make-up of other plant drugs such as aspirin from the willow and morphine from the opium poppy. In 1944, scientists working for the Winthrop Chemical Company in the United States found that garlic cloves contain cells that are rich in alliin, a sulphur-containing version of an amino acid and that separate cells contain the enzyme allinase. Alliin itself has almost no smell or taste, but when a garlic clove is cut or crushed, the cell walls are damaged and alliin and allinase come into contact. This triggers a chemical reaction that forms sulphenic acid, but this is unstable and steadily breaks down into another compound – allicin.

Allicin is also very unstable and once created, it breaks down into other sulphur compounds called sulphides, which are responsible for garlic's arresting aroma. Sulphides are made very quickly if garlic is heated or cooked after crushing, but are made slowly if the crushed garlic is left standing or in the fridge. This is why crushed garlic becomes stronger smelling and stronger tasting the longer it is left. Although the majority of the sulphides have therapeutic properties, these eventually break down into polysulphides, which have no health benefits. Therefore, to take advantage of garlic's health benefits, it is best to eat it as fresh as possible, while allicin is still present.

A clove a day

potassium (aids with correct functioning of heart, muscles and nerves; regulates fluid and mineral balance; helps maintain normal blood pressure)

iron (required for red-blood-cell formation)

selenium and germanium (help boost the immune system and have antioxidant properties)

vitamin B6 (involved in protein metabolism and maintaining healthy nervous system, skin, muscles and blood; boosts immune system)

vitamin C (helps fight infection, assists with absorption of iron from the blood, speeds up wound healing, helps produce collagen and keep gums healthy; important antioxidant, protecting the body from the effect of harmful free radicals and thus helps to reduce the risk of cancer)

Shifting status

In medieval and Renaissance Europe, garlic was a familiar part of life and enormous amounts were grown in monastery gardens alongside other popular herbs and plants. Queen Elizabeth I's herbalist, William Turner, recorded in his paper *A New Herball*: "Garlyke is not only good meat but also good medicine," while in his 1653 book *Complete Herbal* Nicholas Culpeper wrote "Mars owns this herb" and suggested its fiery heat could fight diseases borne from the cold and the wet. He cited garlic as a treatment for countless conditions — bites, boils, cramp, cuts, chest complaints, head colds, jaundice, poison and worms.

However, toward the late 17th century, the burgeoning mercantile class in Protestant northern Europe began to turn their noses up at garlic's earthy pungency, and it was at this time that garlic's use for culinary and medicinal purposes started to part ways. Physic gardens, like Chelsea Physic Garden, established in 1673, multiplied across Europe, proving a continued interest in the medicinal properties of plants. Garlic was still listed as a useful remedy in Jonathan Stokes' *Botanical Materia Medica* in 1812 and yet the growing class distinctions in England at the time were no doubt responsible for its diminished popularity in the kitchen. Strong smells became more objectionable as improved sanitization reached the streets and houses of the urban and wealthy population. Garlic became seen as the food of the lower classes as city folk began to dissociate themselves from the peasant way of life. In 1699, the diarist John Evelyn

wrote of garlic: "We absolutely forbid it entrance into our Salleting [salad], by reason of its intolerable Rankness." And by the time Mrs Beeton wrote her revered publication on household matters in the 1860s, her only references to garlic were: "Unless very sparingly used, the flavor is disagreeable to the English palate" and "The smell of this plant is generally considered offensive… It was in greater repute with our ancestors than it is with ourselves, although it is still used as a seasoning or herb."

While Mediterranean cooking continued to use garlic as a staple flavoring, the dislike of garlic among the Anglo-Saxons spread to the United States, where its popularity is also relatively recent. Not so long ago, pre-1950s, garlic flavors and smells were considered far too stinky and perhaps too ethnic for conservative tastes on both sides of the Atlantic.

However, in the last few decades, a welcome change has emerged. While much of the world never lost their affection for garlic, it has taken on a new acceptance among health-conscious Anglo-Saxon foodies and been firmly taken back into the fold. In our globe-trotting era, we embrace international cuisines, and more exotic flavors and scents are now accepted – even expected – in our kitchens. There's also a preference for natural and organic foods, and more and more people are turning to natural remedies rather than pharmaceutical solutions to improve their health. Garlic is once again where it always should be – at the heart of our homes!

"Garlyke is not only good meat but also good medicine."

William Turner, *A New Herball*

Celebrating garlic

What better excuse to celebrate than garlic! It's a sentiment shared by thousands of alliophiles who each year flock to festivals all over the world to honor the stinking rose. The biggest and best-known fair takes place in the Californian farming town of Gilroy, "the garlic capital of the world." Our own homegrown version of Gilroy is the annual Isle of Wight Garlic Festival. Inspired by a trip to Gilroy, my father Colin established the festival in 1983 as a means to raise money for the local community and village school. In the early years the garlic queen (a role I perhaps too willingly accepted as a teenager) was chased around the arena by a fanged vampire king and had to fend him off with a string of garlic – much to the delight of the crowd!

Ten of the best garlic festivals to visit:

The Gilroy Garlic Festival, Gilroy, California, USA
www.gilroygarlicfestival.com/
The famous Gilroy festival was started in 1979 by Italian resident Rudy Melone, who convinced local farmers to host an annual celebration of their crop. It has since raised millions of dollars for local charities.

The Isle of Wight Garlic Festival, Newchurch, Isle of Wight, UK
www.garlic-festival.co.uk/
Huge marquees offer all manner of tempting food and drink, including garlic beer and garlic ice cream, as well as cooking demos, tastings, and displays of our acclaimed Isle of Wight garlic bulbs.

La Fête de l'Ail Rose, Lautrec, France
www.ailrosedelautrec.com/
A celebration of Lautrec's pink garlic takes place on the first Friday of August every year. Highlights include free tastings of the region's traditional pink garlic soup, and competitions for the longest garlic bunch and best garlic tart.

La Foire à l'Ail Fumé d'Arleux, Arleux, France
This three-day event is dedicated to Arleux's specialty – smoked garlic. Distinguished by a deep golden color and smoky aroma, Arleux garlic was originally smoked over a peat fire to preserve it, allowing it to be stored for up to a year.

L'Aglio di Voghiera, Voghiera, Ferrara, Italy
www.agliodivoghiera.com/
In the grounds of the Castello del Belriguardo, fair-goers can sample garlic gelato and classic Ferrarese raviolis with cheese and garlic. There's also a garlic-braiding seminar.

Tasköprü International Culture and Garlic Festival, Tasköprü, Turkey
As the country's main garlic producer, the small historical town of Tasköprü each year hosts a large garlic fair that includes cooking contests, folk dances and horse races.

Hudson Valley Garlic Festival, Saugerties, New York, USA
www.hudsonvalleygarlic.com/
Taking place at the end of September at the foot of the Catskill Mountains, the event includes chef demonstrations and lectures on a wide range of garlic-related topics.

Elephant Garlic Festival, North Plains, Oregon, USA
www.funstinks.com/
"Fun stinks" is the motto of this hugely popular annual gathering, which crowns a garlic king and queen.

Southern Vermont Garlic & Herb Festival, Bennington, Vermont, USA
www.lovegarlic.com/
Claiming to raise "the biggest stink in Vermont," this annual festival offers foods and crafts, garlic planting, braiding and cooking demos – and garlic golf!

Hills Garlic Festival, Centennial Park, New Denver, British Columbia, Canada
www.hillsgarlicfest.ca/
A huge fundraising community event that includes a Heaviest Clove contest and a poetry competition for those inspired to write their own ode to the clove.

Varieties and growing

The wonderful world of garlic

You might think that one bulb of garlic is very like another, but you would be wrong. In fact there are literally hundreds of garlic varieties in the world and almost all differ in size, color, shape, flavor, pungency, number of cloves, storage times and even ease of peeling. Most people are unaware of this as they seldom see more than one kind in the supermarket or grocer's. Yet if you buy from a farmers' market or a specialist grower, you will be amazed at the huge selection available – certainly most people who shop at The Garlic Farm are – and from there you will never look back.

The good news is that all this variety is readily available to you since the best way to enter the wonderful world of garlic is to grow your own. It is one of the easiest crops you can grow and you will be richly rewarded. The satisfaction of harvesting your very own high-quality bulbs is second to none, not to mention the benefit of having a flavorful organic crop right on your doorstep, and you will discover the satisfying ritual of retaining cloves from your best bulbs for next year's planting stock. You can grow garlic in your vegetable patch, flowerbed or even in pots on your patio or window ledge. From planting to harvest takes up to nine months and when the beautiful white heads are teased from Mother Earth, you'll feel like a proud new parent.

Varieties

In the absence of a universal naming system, the classification of garlic varieties is somewhat complicated and confusing. Many have been renamed over the centuries, so although they may be genetically identical, they have unique country or regional names. At The Garlic Farm, for example, we have selected more than 20 varieties with memorable labels such as Lautrec Wight, Provence Wight and Tuscany Wight that give a clear indication of their native land. However, all varieties can basically be divided into two types or subspecies: hardnecks (*Ophioscorodon* or *ophios* for short) and softnecks (*Sativum*). The following diagram is a simplification of garlic's classification to illustrate the variation across different subspecies.

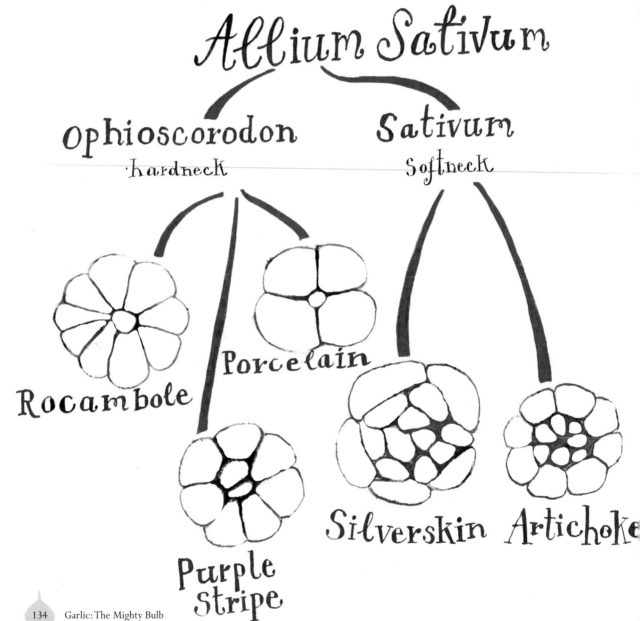

Allium Sativum

Ophioscorodon
hardneck

Sativum
Softneck

Rocambole

Porcelain

Purple Stripe

Silverskin

Artichoke

Hardnecks

Hardneck or "bolting garlic" gets its name from a stiff flower stalk, or scape, which is best removed to maximize bulb size (see page 144). Hardnecks originated in the mountains of Central Asia and are more winter-friendly, making them suitable for northern climates. They have a looser outer wrapper than softnecks do, and they produce fewer, larger cloves with a stronger flavor. There are three distinct groups, each containing many varieties that produce differing results, depending on climate, soil type and other growing conditions:

Rocambole

Often considered to be the "gourmet" garlic due to its superior taste, Rocambole is the most widely grown of the hardneck group. Its tan-colored cloves are easy to peel, making it extremely popular with chefs, but unfortunately it doesn't store well. In spring Rocamboles grow a scape that coils into a distinctive double loop before straightening, giving them the nickname "serpent" garlic. Varieties include Spanish Roja, Rose de Lautrec (Toulouse, south-west France) and Spanish Morado.

Porcelain

The tallest of the hardneck group, Porcelains can reach up to 2.1 m (6 ft) and have attractive large, white bulbs, occasionally streaked with purple or brown. They produce very few cloves – sometimes as little as four – which makes them expensive to grow as a quarter of your crop will have to be set aside for next season's planting stock. However, they contain the highest levels of allicin, making them the healthiest of all garlics, which have a hot, strong flavor. They are tolerant of cold and store quite well, but may need more watering in the late stages of growth. In spring Porcelains produce scapes that coil, snake-like, in all directions before straightening. Varieties include Music (Eastern Europe) and Georgian Crystal.

Artichoke

Artichoke garlic is most favored by commercial growers as it produces good plants with relatively few problems. It grows well in a wide range of climates, it is popular with novice growers too. Artichoke garlic is also harvested early, with large bulbs that store well. Plants have a row of 12–20 outer cloves and a row of smaller inner cloves. Flavor can vary quite dramatically, but generally they taste milder than Silverskins. Varieties include California Early, Iberian Wight (south-west Spain) and Provence Wight (Drôme Valley, Provence, France).

Silverskin

Silverskins are favored for their excellent storage capacity, rich flavor and tolerance to a wide range of growing conditions. They are harvested later, so it is generally best to harvest them well into the summer months. Their smooth, silvery white bulbs tend to contain more cloves than any other garlic group, and their long, sturdy, pliable necks make them the best choice for braiding (see pages 147–149). Our favorite Silverskin variety is Solent Wight, from the Auvergne region in central France. We have developed this to grow particularly well in the Isle of Wight climate, and it makes up the majority of our garlic crop. Other varieties include Venetian, Picardy and California Late.

Purple Stripe

These beautiful garlic plants have bulb wrappers with purplish stripes, hence their name – some are almost solid purple. Also renowned for their rich flavor, Purple Stripes are considered to be the best types for roasting. The clove skins are thin and closely attached to the bulb, so they are more difficult to peel but can be stored longer than Rocamboles. They produce a scape which, if allowed to develop will produce pink or purple flowers. Varieties include Red Sicilian and Purple Moldovan (Moldova).

Softnecks

Softnecks or "non-bolting" garlic does not usually produce a flowering stalk, although if stressed it is possible for some varieties to partially bolt. Softnecks are less tolerant of the cold weather than hardnecks, making them better suited to warmer climates. They also store longer and travel better, which is why they are commonly grown for commercial use. There are two main groups, but, as with hardnecks, varieties within these groups differ immensely:

Elephant garlic

Although elephant garlic looks like a super-sized version of normal garlic, it is, in fact, a member of the leek family (*Allium ampeloprasum*) and not really a garlic at all. Its enormous bulbs are something of a novelty and contain several large cloves that have a very mild flavor, with none of the pungency of *Allium sativum,* but they are also good to cook with (see page 19). Sometimes the cloves don't divide, producing a slightly larger single-clove (solo) bulb. This can be harvested or planted again the following season, when it will often produce segmented cloves. Elephant garlic needs a long, warm growing season to grow well, and produces a long straight stem with an attractive large flower head, making it a popular garden plant.

Growing

Nothing beats the buzz of excitement in our farmyard when the first bulbs of the season appear. As piles of them arrive on a trailer, ready to be dried, cleaned, clipped and braided, we marvel at their beauty. Maybe we're deluded by our love of the crop, but they do seem to become more attractive each year, and no doubt garlic growers the world over share in this wonderment at nature's bounty.

The first step toward achieving good results is to make sure you obtain good-quality planting stock. You can try planting any garlic cloves that are available to you, but it's best to acquire clean seed stock from a garden center or mail-order supplier as garlic purchased from a supermarket or grocery shop may have been treated or stored in a way that is detrimental to its growing potential. At The Garlic Farm we offer a large choice of varieties for planting, as well as growing. All our garlic is available online, where you will also find other suppliers of various types of garlic seed bulbs.

When to plant

The best time to plant will depend on the type of plant you are growing. Some garlic varieties are best planted early in the autumn and others later in the autumn or in the spring. As a general rule, for best results plant about three weeks before the ground freezes – usually early to mid-autumn. If you have purchased stock from a supplier, it should include a growing guide with an indication of the best planting time – some varieties fare better if planted in the spring, for example. If you're planting late, don't worry. As long as the cloves are in the ground any time up to late spring, you should get some results, although your bulbs may be on the small side.

Garlic in its natural environment

Garlic's wild habitat is on mountain slopes, emerging just below the snow line in early spring. Watered by a constant trickle of melting snow through its roots, the life cycle of garlic has evolved around the availability of this slow but constant natural irrigation through the spring months. The water diminishes as summer arrives, so bulb growth ceases and aging begins. The bulb dries and goes to sleep until reawakened by its physiological clock in response to winter's cold, followed by warmer moist conditions the following spring.

"As a general rule, for best results plant about three weeks before the ground freezes – usually early to mid-autumn."

Preparing the ground

Positioning

Garlic will grow in the shade, but it loves the sun, so ideally choose the sunniest position possible. If you're planting in a vegetable garden, try to select an area that hasn't contained members of the onion family (chives, leeks, onions, spring onions, shallots, garlic) for at least two years in order to minimize the risk of disease.

Companion planting

The naturally occurring sulfur in garlic can act as a fungicide and pesticide that can benefit other plants in your garden. For this reason, plant your garlic close to virtually any other vegetable and it will help to deter aphids and other common pests. It can be especially effective at keeping bugs away from lettuce and cabbage and many gardeners rely on garlic in their rose beds to fend off aphids.

Soil

For a good crop of big, healthy bulbs, a rich, fertile soil is important. Work with whatever you have in your garden and simply add nutrients to make it more garlic-friendly. Spreading some compost before planting can avoid the classic symptoms of yellowing, poor vigor and small bulbs. As with all garden plants, a free-draining but moisture-retentive soil with a pH of above 6.7 is ideal. Garlic doesn't like sitting in the wet, so add sandy gravel to improve drainage in heavy clay soil and add lime to make acidic soils more alkaline.

Most garden soils already have good supplies of phosphate and potash from previous fertilizing efforts. Garlic appears to respond well to applications of sulphate of potash. It helps make plants stronger and more disease-resistant.

To prepare the soil for planting, dig and turn over the topsoil to a spade's depth. Work it down so you have a fine top layer of at least 4cm.

How to plant

When you're ready to plant, and not before, break up the bulb into individual cloves, taking care not to damage them (as this can lead to rotting) and discard any unhealthy cloves. If your bulb is already broken up into cloves, it's not a disaster, but they do keep better as whole bulbs.

Draw out a furrow 3–4 cm (1 in) deep. Make sure you plant the cloves root end down, tip pointing up, and deep enough so they can be covered with 3–4 cm (1 in) of loose soil, measured from the clove tip. Place

the cloves so they are just resting in the soil at the bottom of the hole or furrow. Large cloves should be spaced 15 cm (5 in) apart, small cloves 10 cm (3 in) apart.

When the whole row is planted, draw the soil over the cloves to cover them completely. If the soil is dry, water sparingly.

In a pot

If you are planting in containers, allow 3 cloves per 15 cm (5 in) pot. A period of cold is necessary to vernalize the clove and trigger the mechanism that induces it to split into cloves and bulb up, so don't leave your plants for too long in the warmth. If you wish, you can bring your garlic plants indoors in the spring and, provided they are in good light and well watered, they should grow well with possibly an earlier harvest than an outdoor crop.

Tending your crop

Up to two months after planting, you will see green shoots emerging. Autumn planting is slower to emerge than spring (which puts on a growth spurt to catch the warmth and sun). In early spring, sprinkle 100g sulphate of potash per square meter or inch around the emerging shoots and lightly hoe or fork it in, taking care not to disturb the plants.

For the remainder of the growth period, all you need to do is keep the plants free of weeds and prevent the ground from drying out. The bulbs should be well watered from late spring onward (during dry weather). If the plants are too dry, the bulbs will be smaller. Do this until a week before harvest, at which point they must be allowed to dry out as this helps the transition from growth to storage.

Pests and diseases

Despite garlic's incredible power to defend itself against many pests, pathogenic fungi and bacteria, the pungent sulphur compounds created by the interaction of its component chemicals is not a deterrent to all types of pest and infection. Your bulbs may succumb to one of the following problems and so here is some advice to help identify, avoid and remedy these issues.

Rust (*Puccinia porri*) can appear as small yellow or orange blisters on the leaves of the plant from early summer onward. Infection comes from spores carried from leeks, chives and other host species in the vicinity. To protect against rust try watering or spraying with sulphur compounds and increasing the levels of sulfate of potash hoed into the ground around the bulbs in early spring. At the first signs of any rust pustules on the leaves, paint them with alcohol (cheap gin will do). For heavy infestations, carefully remove infected leaves and destroy them, painting rust with alcohol where it occurs on only a few leaves. There are several commercial anti-fungal and rust products available at garden centers that offer some protection against rust. Prevention is key as once you have rust on your plants it will be very difficult to cure.

Onion fly is typically recognizable by halted growth and a thickening of the neck of the plant, which causes the plant to die. The onion fly lays its eggs close to or on the plant. When hatched, the maggot bores into the bulb bringing bacteria with it, which causes rot and eventual bulb collapse. If plants die for no apparent reason around late spring/early summer, lift an affected plant and look for a fat maggot inside. To protect against onion fly, keep the soil around the plants well cultivated in early spring.

White rot (*Sclerotium cepivorum*) is a fungus and poses the most serious threat to garlic crops all over the world. The first signs of infection appear in the form of a white, cottony-looking fungal growth apparent around the base and up the sides of the bulbs, with tiny black globules, like poppy seeds, appearing among the fungus. Eventually, all foliage will die and the bulbs decay. If you are unfortunate enough to come across this problem, you should destroy all affected material and alliums should not be grown on the infected site for at least 15 years. White rot can occur where there is a history of continuous allium cultivation on the same site. Other plants are not affected.

Eelworm is invisible to the naked eye and could be mistaken for white rot or onion fly. It is a soil-borne nematode hosted by a number of plants around the garden. The leaves of infected plants may turn yellow and die and, where infection is more severe, the bulb may deteriorate completely. To avoid eelworm, it is wise to follow routine

practices of rotating crops. Also, as eelworms are most commonly spread through infected planting stock since they can survive in the stored plant tissues, do not use any planting stock with signs of deterioration and avoid using composted garlic debris on garlic planting sites.

To reduce the risk of pests and disease attacking your garlic crop, follow these basic principles:
- Rotate your crop: wait at least 3 years before planting in the same bed. In between, plant non-allium crops.
- Avoid an over-supply of nitrogen to the soil.
- Take care to use clean and healthy planting stock, selecting only the most healthy-looking bulbs.
- Do not use compost from garlic debris on garlic planting beds.
- Dry your garlic well after harvest.
- Carefully remove all garlic stems and leaves from the beds after harvest.

Removing scapes

A few weeks before harvest time, hardneck varieties will bolt, producing a flowering stem, or scape, which emerges from the top of the plant. The stem twists and curls attractively, known as a rocambole, on the end of which is the flower head, suspended above the leaf canopy. The scape bud can appear within a matter of days, and within a week it will be held on a stem above the leaf canopy.

To direct the plant's energies into producing a larger bulb, cut off the rocambole once it has formed. This can increase the bulb size by as much as 50 percent. The scapes and stem also make a unique and incredibly tasty culinary treat (see page 60). If the scape is left intact, the bud will eventually burst open into a purple flower head with tiny bulbs, or bulbils. These can be planted but with very unreliable results, sometimes taking years to produce a bulb.

Harvesting

The optimum time to harvest softneck varieties is as soon as the plant stems begin to lie horizontal on the ground. For hardnecks, wait until 30 percent of the crop's leaves turn dry or yellow. Both these signs indicate that the growing cycle is completed, the bulbs have reached full size and are ready to lift. Leaving your garlic in the ground unharvested results in grey, stained bulbs and eventually shortens its shelf life.

Then comes the exciting bit. Lift your garlic carefully from the soil, loosening the earth around the bulbs if necessary. Brush off the excess dirt before laying them in a tray, then dry them in the sun or in a dry, well-ventilated place. If the weather is dry and hot, the bulbs can be laid out in the garden, but it's probably best to put them in a greenhouse, conservatory or simply undercover and leave them for a few weeks. You'll know when the garlic is completely dry because there will be no greenness left in the stem and the outer layers of skin will brush off easily – this can take a few weeks. Alternatively, of course, you can eat the garlic before it has completely dried or even immediately after harvesting as green or wet garlic – use it like a spring onion (see page 19). Remember to keep the stems of your drying garlic intact if you intend to braid it into strings or weave it into grappes (small bunches) for storage.

Storage

Garlic will store well in a range of conditions, but it is important not to let it get too cold – never keep it in the fridge as this will encourage it to sprout early. A dry, warmish environment is best, and the most beautiful and convenient way to store it is in strings or grappes, which can be hung in your kitchen. Not only are they attractive, they also help the bulbs last longer by allowing air to circulate around them. They're relatively easy to make too, provided you are equipped with a strong pair of hands and a fair amount of patience. Just follow the step-by-step instructions below.

Garlic string

You will need:

- 10 or more fully dried garlic bulbs with stems intact
- raffia or garden string
- a pair of pruning shears

1. Clean the bulbs by using your thumb to brush off the outer layer of skin, then trim the roots with the shears. Be careful not to cut the actual flesh of the garlic (or your fingers).

2. Arrange the bulbs in pairs of similar size.

3. Select the two largest bulbs – these will form the base of the plait. Wrap the stem of one bulb tightly around the other, as close to bulb necks as possible.

4. Holding these two bulbs in place, take a third bulb from the next smallest pair and place it at the center. Take the protruding stem and wrap it around the stem base of the third bulb.

5. Take the fourth bulb and place it next to its pair, then hold it in place by wrapping the stem to the left into the middle.

6. Continue to add bulbs in this way, always pulling the braid as tight as possible while you add each one.

7. When all the bulbs have been added, continue to braid the stems for a few centimeters (inches), then finish off by tying the tops with raffia or garden string. Make a loop for hanging, then use the shears to trim off any stray bits of stem or roots.

Garlic grappe

You will need:

• any number or size of bulbs – I usually find about 6 to 9 bulbs look most attractive
• good-quality raffia; if not, garden string
• a pair of pruning shears

Making a garlic grappe is an easy way to present and store your garlic.

1. Cut a generous 1.5 m (4 ft) length of raffia or string. Take the largest bulb and wrap the raffia around the stem as close to the bulb as possible, tying it at one end.

2. Take another bulb and place it next to the first one. Wrap the raffia around the stem, close to the bulb, then around both stems a couple of times, pulling them tightly together. You should be able to make it quite tight without breaking.

3. Continue to add bulbs, wrapping the raffia around the newly added stem, then around all the stems until you have what looks like a bouquet of garlic.

The family business

Large-scale garlic production is a labor-intensive process that requires harvesting, curing and storing to be done almost exclusively by hand. The garlic is lifted from the soil by a mechanized harvester then taken to large glasshouses to dry before being cleaned bulb by bulb. It is then woven into strings or grappes, a process my siblings and I have all been involved in. As teenagers we spent our summers sitting outside the glasshouse, earning pocket money at a rate of a few cents per clean bulb – and a few more cents for a completed braid or grappe. We'd race to complete as many as possible, ending the summer with strong but rough, calloused hands. Needless to say, braiding garlic has become a rather competitive sport in the Boswell household and we've created exacting standards for our braids – no slackness or floppy bulbs allowed!

4. Once you have added an adequate number of bulbs (6–9 works well), continue to wrap the raffia tightly around the stems in a spiral for about 12 cm (4 in), then finish off and make a loop with the raffia for hanging. Use the shears to trim any stray bits of stem or roots.

Garlic FAQs

At The Garlic Farm shop, we try to answer all our customers' questions about cooking, growing and using garlic for health, no matter how obscure. Everything from "Can you grow smoked garlic?" to "Can I take it in my hand luggage?"…we've heard it all. Most of these topics are dealt with in detail in this book, but here are the quick reference answers to our most commonly asked questions.

How long will garlic last?

This will largely depend on where you bought your garlic and how it has been stored up to the time of purchase. The garlic we sell most of for culinary use is Solent Wight, which has a particularly lengthy storage capacity. It is usually still fine for use up to 9 months after harvest, provided it has been stored in dry, light conditions and not too cold. Unfortunately, much of the garlic sold in the supermarkets has been stored in cold storage, meaning that within a few weeks of coming into ambient temperatures, it will think spring has arrived and begin to sprout, so it will not last so long. If you buy garlic from a specialist supplier or from your local farmers' market, ask when it was harvested and then expect it to last for a few months from that time.

Can you grow garlic from a seed?

Garlic can rarely be grown from a seed produced by the flower. To grow garlic you simply have to break up a bulb and plant the individual cloves. If you intend to plant garlic, it is best to buy stock specifically intended to be used for planting. Garlic, like all *alliums*, is susceptible to viruses. By buying garlic from a private supplier it will more likely be virus-free, as commercial growers will have grown their product from a seed via meristem culture in laboratory conditions to avoid passing down viruses. This process can take from five to seven years.

How many years can you continue to plant from the same stock?

As long as it continues to grow and produce satisfactory bulbs. The only risk of continuing to plant from the same stock is that your garlic will be more prone to viruses and disease such as white rot or eel worm (nematodes).

Will it make my kitchen smell?

Only in a good way! In fact, as long as the bulbs remain intact and undamaged, they will give off very little odor. It is only when you start to crush, chop or in some way damage the clove during cooking preparation that you start to smell garlic's distinctive odor. Then your kitchen will be filled with that wonderful, unmistakeable aroma of garlic cooking.

Does it keep vampires away?

Of course it does. Garlic's reputation for repelling evil spirits is probably its biggest claim to fame. The popularization of this claim is largely thanks to Bram Stoker's portrayal of Count Dracula in his bestselling novel. Dracula appears to be easily repelled by garlic. Never mind that Stoker had never set foot in Dracula's Transylvania, the idea has definitely stuck. However, Stoker was not the first to attribute these powers to garlic. References to garlic as a deterrent against evil can be found in much ancient folklore. Hang a bulb of garlic in your kitchen window and your house will remain free from bloodsucking creatures!

Can I eat it if I'm taking warfarin?

Eating garlic as part of one's normal diet, in cooked form, will not diminish the effect of anticoagulants like warfarin. However some medical professionals have expressed concern as to the effects of eating large quantities of raw garlic in conjunction with warfarin. Consult your physician before using raw garlic while on warfarin.

Do I put the whole bulb in the ground to grow it?

One of the most commonly asked questions from novice growers. No, break it into its constituent cloves and plant the cloves. The only time one might plant whole bulbs is when planting "solo" bulbs of Elephant or other garlic types that did not divide the previous year (usually due to a lack of a cold shock. This can happen from a late planting in March/April).

How do I prevent rust forming on the leaves of my garlic plants?

Rust is spread on the air from other host plants in surrounding gardens and countryside. Warm, moist conditions will encourage it. No reliable cure for rust exists so it's best to concentrate on prevention. I'd recommend feeding plants with sulphate of potash in February and also spraying the leaves with Sulphur from April onward, every 10 days or so. This will result in strong plants that will be less susceptible.

Resources

Purchase British garlic for eating and growing from:

The Garlic Farm on the Isle of Wight

www.thegarlicfarm.co.uk

+44 1983 865378

Garlic and seed for growing can also be purchased from these suppliers:

Gourmet Garlic Gardens: www.gourmetgarlicgardens.com

Boundary Garlic Farms: www.garlicfarm.ca

Hood River Garlic: www.hoodrivergarlic.com

2 Sisters Garlic: www.2sistersgarlic.com

Grey Duck Garlic: www.greyduckgarlic.com

Filaree Garlic Farm: www.filareefarm.com

For the latest information on the medicinal benefits of garlic: www.garlic-central.com

Further reading

There are a number of books whose information I have drawn on to explain the health benefits of garlic.

If you are interested in finding out more, here are some suggestions:

Fulder, S. *The Garlic Book, Nature's Powerful Healer* Avery Publishing Group, 1997

Pacurar, M and Krejci, G. *Garlic Consumption and Health* Nova Science Publishers, 2010

Koch H.P. and Lawson L.D. *The Science and the Therapeutic Application of Allium Sativum L. and Related Species* Baltimore MD: Williams and Wilkins, 1996

For an in-depth analysis of garlic varieties and their classification, see:

Meredith, T.J. *The Complete Book of Garlic: A Guide For Gardeners, Growers and Serious Cooks* Timber Press, 2008

Photo credits

cover: DL Pohl / Shutterstock, p. 6 Lisa Linder, p. 12 (left) Liz Gregg, p. 13 (left) Liz Gregg, p. 16 Laurence Mouton / PhotoAlto / Corbis, p. 18 (top) Robert Harding World Imagery / Corbis, (bottom) Imagemore Co., Ltd / Imagemore Co., Ltd. / Corbis, p. 24 Ocean / Corbis, p. 90 Bettmann / Corbis, p. 91 Gary Cralle / Getty Images p. 92 Diego Rodriguez de Silva y Velasquez / Bridgeman / Getty Images, p. 94 Time & Life Pictures / Getty Images, p. 100 Thelma & Louise / the food passionates / Corbis, p. 103 Science Photo Library, p. 107 Science Photo Library, p. 108 Martin Benik / Westend61 / Corbis, p. 115 Gavin Kingcome Photography / Getty Images, p. 118 (top) Carl Mydans / Time Life Pictures / Getty Images, (left) ChinaFotoPress / Getty Images, (bottom) Devendra M Singh / AFP / Getty Images, p. 119 (top) Narinder Nanu / AFP / Getty Images, (bottom) Keystone-France / Gamma-Keystone via Getty Images, p. 122 Science Photo Library, p. 123 Ocean / Corbis, p. 124 David Harrigan / ableimages / Corbis, p. 125 (top) David Harrigan / ableimages / Corbis, (bottom) Meng Zhongde / Xinhua Press / Corbis, p. 126 (top) Lucas van Valckenborch / The Bridgeman Art Collection, (bottom) Alinari / Alinari Archives, Florence / Alinari via Getty Images, p. 127 Martin Engelbrecht / The Bridgeman Art Collection, p. 128 Tony Linck / Time & Life Pictures / Getty Images, p. 151 Boyer / Roger Viollet / Getty Images, p. 188 Time & Life Pictures / Getty Images, p. 160 Popperfoto / Getty Images

Index

Acknowledgments

With thanks:

To all my tasters and testers of everything from the sweet and delicious to the extremely experimental.

Special thanks to my husband, Barnes, for his unfailing support and my children Arlo and Freya
for already being able to recognize a good garlic bulb.

To my dear friend and excellent cook, Columbine Mulvey for all her expert help, culinary tips, ideas and inspiration.

To my parents, without whom this book would not have been possible, for so many reasons
other than the obvious. Thank you both.

To Kyle, Judith and Vicki at Kyle Books for all their hard work and their faith in this book.

To everyone at The Garlic Farm. Keep up the good work!